D0959343

Organize
FOR A Fresh Start

Organize
FOR A Fresh Start

Embrace Your Next Chapter in Life

Susan Fay West

BETTERWAY HOME
CINCINNATI, OHIO
WWW.BETTERWAYBOOKS.COM

ORGANIZE FOR A FRESH START. Copyright © 2011 by Susan Fay West. Manufactured in China. All rights reserved. No part of this book may be reproduced in any form or by any electronic or mechanical means including information storage and retrieval systems without permission in writing from the publisher, except by a reviewer who may quote brief passages in a review. Published by Betterway Home, an imprint of F+W Media, Inc., 4700 East Galbraith Road, Cincinnati, Ohio, 45236. (800) 289-0963. First Edition.

Other fine Betterway Home books are available from your local bookstore and online suppliers. Visit our website at www.betterwayhome.com.

15 14 13 12 11   5 4 3 2 1

ISBN-13: 978-1-4403-0852-9

Distributed in Canada by Fraser Direct
100 Armstrong Avenue
Georgetown, Ontario, Canada L7G 5S4
Tel: (905) 877-4411

Distributed in the U.K. and Europe by F&W Media International, LTD
Brunel House, Forde Close, Newton Abbot, TQ12 4PU, UK
Tel: (+44) 1626 323200, Fax: (+44) 1626 323319
E-mail: enquiries@fwmedia.com

Distributed in Australia by Capricorn Link
P.O. Box 704, S. Windsor NSW, 2756 Australia
Tel: (02) 4577-3555

Edited by Jacqueline Musser; Designed by Clare Finney;
Production coordinated by Mark Griffin

ABOUT THE AUTHOR

Sue West lives on a lake with her lifelong friend, Donna, her Entlebucher Swiss Mountain dog, Sanford (born in the same year as her organizing business), a gaggle of geese, one lone lake turtle, and a few other animal friends. In a period of roughly eighteen months, she struggled through more than a few major life changes and transitions, and  came out quite happy on the other side. Organizing was a key player along the way of course. And so it became her passion to assist others at midlife and beyond, to move on from change, taking the best along for the journey into the next chapter of life.

Sue owns Space4U, Organizing Services, LLC, independently. She is a Certified Organizer Coach® and Certified Professional Organizer®. Through organizing services, classes, and organizing coaching, Sue works with people in their second half of life to downsize, organize, and simplify their life, their belongings, and their time. Her specialty is supporting clients through change and transitions, such as downsizing, loss of a partner/spouse, health issues, adult ADHD diagnosis, caregiving, the empty-nest stage, pre-retirement, and into retirement.

She also holds specialty certificates in life transitions, ADHD, and chronic disorganization from the Institute for Challenging Disorganization and is currently pursuing her level three certification from the ICD. She has an MBA from Babson College, Massachusetts, and a BA from Smith College, Massachusetts.

DEDICATION

To DMB, who asked, "Are you happy?"
On a snowy walk around the lake.
And when I answered that question, my fresh start began.

ACKNOWLEDGMENTS

You'll read in the first chapter about my story, what led me to write this book, and why organizing is so important as we move through the transitions of life.

Here, I honor individuals who have shared their wisdom with me. They have gently pushed me to be the person I was meant to become as I moved through my transitions. And they have shown me what I have to give to those around me. Your inspiration, support, and belief in me and my abilities to get this book written was instrumental in sharing expertise with people I've never met.

And to my readers, some of these are professionals you may want to seek out yourself.

To Donna, my biggest supporter from the beginning, believing I had more to offer than I even understood, and who believed in me unconditionally. You are a treasure of a unique kind.

To Roberta, who came up to the lake to give me a cooking lesson and suggested I check out "those organizing shows" on TV because I'd be great at it.

To Denslow Brown, who realized coaching skills needed to come to the organizing industry and built The Coach Approach program and Organizer Coach Certification. As a coach and mentor, you've asked insightful and creative questions. Your friendship arrived at a perfect time in my life.

To Robin Warren, website designer and friend, who often enough complimented my writing and encouraged me to do more with it.

To my clients: You are amazing. You learn about yourselves. I learn from you. You share what you may not have shared with others. I am honored to support you through your transitions. You have made me better in my chosen career in the second chapter of my life.

To Jacqueline Musser, my book editor. Jackie's been my book shepherd and editor, believing in the value of what I write about, believing in my writing abilities, gently delivering suggestions for improvement or clarity, and being so organized about it all! Most important, you allowed me to write and took care of everything else, which is exactly how I wanted to do this. I respect your talents tremendously.

To the Institute for Challenging Disorganization, an extraordinary resource for organizing professionals as well as for the public. This group really understands what organizing is about for people, and demonstrates that through its education, membership, and service to the public and our profession. Thank you for constantly raising the bar so we can be better and better for our clients.

To my cribbage crew: We all need support as we move through life changes. Wednesday nights, after school, for pizza and red wine and lots of life conversations was just what I needed as my life changed.

To the Enos family, who has shown me a different face of family: I'm so thrilled you have been in my life; "you don't have to be crazy to be in this family, but it sure doesn't hurt!"

To my closest friends today: What would I do without you? You are my extended family. Your support and love shows me what friendship is really about.

To my grandmothers. Strong, independent, and wise women, they went to college in the days when women weren't supposed to. Both inspired me in different ways, and still do today.

To my aunt Fay, who passed away this year. One of the most authentic, genuine people I have been blessed to know. Rebellious, funny, and unconditional in her love—all qualities I continue to aspire to make my own. Heaven is a lucky place.

To my family: You raised me with strength, independence, and a sense of humor. My curiosity for learning started with you. My adaptability and interest in connecting with people started with you. Thank you for being who you are.

contents

Your life is full of different chapters. As you move through these chapters, priorities change, as does your mind-set about your belongings and your schedule and activities. When this shift happens, it's time to reorganize.

Before you begin a journey, you need to know your destination. This chapter helps you create a vision of your newly reorganized life so you know what you are working toward.

Whether you're new to organizing or have organized in the past, the Three Ps help you create and maintain systems that meet your specific needs.

What's holding you back from reaching your organizing goals? This chapter is full of encouragement and ideas to help you get started and stick with your reorganizing efforts.

You're ready to begin, but where? This chapter takes you through each room of your home and helps you create a plan.

Organizing is all about making decisions—what to let go of and what to keep. This chapter helps you make no-regrets decisions so everything in your home enhances your new chapter in life.

Introduction

YOUR LIFE IS IN TRANSITION NOW. While change is difficult, that place in between the old chapter and the new chapter—the before and the after— is even more difficult. It's a place of limbo where you're not through the changes and you're not quite into your new chapter.

Organizing is so helpful in dealing with life's big events. It's not simply a "nice to have"—it's an essential practice. The benefits of staying organized during and after major life changes are numerous.

- Organizing is cathartic and can help you process your emotions. As you go through your things, you're not only thinking about whether to keep or let go of items, you're thinking about the transition itself, the emotions, what you'll do next, how you're managing.

- Organizing gives you a sense of control, which, in the context of a life transition, is at a shortage, or may not even exist at some points. At midcrisis we often have no control.

- Organizing allows you to use your energy on the transition and the emotions of it. It gets you moving and makes you an agent of positive change in your home. You are no longer a passive bystander.

- Organizing focuses you on what's really important as you move into the transition, while you're in it, and as you move out of it and into your next chapter of life.

I coach my clients that organizing is part of your support system, whether you're clearing the clutter, reorganizing, or changing how you use your time.

And in the words of coaching and organizing clients, organizing your stuff, time, and/or space . . .

- Helps clear the fog.
- Helps you put your life back together.
- Helps put your new life together.
- Helps you let go more easily when you know what's important to keep.
- Helps you visualize the new place you're headed more easily.

This book will help you step-by-step to reap the full benefits of organizing during a life transition. Work through things at your own pace. Call a friend for support if you need it. Step away when you need to and come back when you are ready.

Let's begin this journey to reorganize your home and your schedule. We will move through this together.

PART ONE

Getting Started

GETTING STARTED IS THE FIRST CHALLENGE TO AN ORGANIZING PROJECT. While you're going through a major life transition, it's difficult to focus on your regular day-to-day life, including housework and keeping things organized. When the dust settles, you may find yourself surrounded by your past—your belongings or home reflect who you were before your transition, but now things have changed. It's time to reorganize.

When we're in sync with our surroundings, we're so much more at peace, and that's why it's important that your home reflect who you are becoming. So how can you get started making your home your own again? How can you create time to tackle this useful and cathartic project? How will you know what you want? In this section you'll gain insight on how to figure out your individual organizing goals as well as how to assess your existing organizing systems to see whether they are still working well for you, even after all you've been through.

1. Live Your Life in Chapters

LIFE IS FULL OF CHANGES—both expected and unexpected, self-imposed and imposed by others. I never expected to own my own business. I never expected to get separated and end up in a divorce. I didn't know I'd be living back at home for a while in my early forties (but thank goodness for Mom and Dad). Changing religions? Nope, also unexpected. I also moved to a different state, became a motor-home owner, and experienced a significant change in my work life from working with clients to working on products. In about eighteen months, a total of nine major changes took place in my life.

Changes, no matter what their nature, interrupt our lives and often require a response because these changes and transitions leave us with homes, belongings, and schedules that no longer work for us. Something is out of alignment, and we're not sure what—often it turns out to be our surroundings, our organizing systems (how we do what we do), or our schedules. Suddenly these systems seem to work against us instead of with us, even if they once fit beautifully into our lives. What worked before will not work now. Responsibilities that didn't exist, or once belonged to someone else, now belong only to you, and you need to find ways to handle them.

Today, life is more complex than it was forty or fifty years ago, when I was growing up. The pace of change is faster. We raise a family, send our kids to college, and then welcome visits from grandchildren. We switch jobs, change careers, go back to school, and retire from one career to pursue a second career. We enjoy years with a spouse or committed partner and then find ourselves single—whether by choice or by other circumstances. We reach an age where our parents begin to depend on us more than we depend on them and roles reverse. Some people call these seasons of life or phases of life. I call them chapters in life.

Just as a book has chapters, our lives do, too. We go through different life stages and circumstances, each of which is a chapter. We don't all have the same set of chapters, but odds are good your life is full of several different chapters. At the very least you transitioned from childhood to teenage years to adulthood, and from school to the working world. Other chapters may include marriage or a life partnership, parenthood, corporate career, self-employment, empty nesting, singleness, grandchildren, retirement, continuing education as an adult, a second career, and caregiving.

Changes, no matter what their nature, interrupt our lives and often require a response because these changes and transitions leave us with homes, belongings, and schedules that no longer work for us.

Each chapter brings new responsibilities and priorities, and you may find your values shift as well. These new circumstances often will give you a different mind-set about your "stuff"—your belongings and your schedule and activities, and that's the key connection to organizing. Your life has changed and your attitude has changed. Now you need to reorganize your belongings and schedule to reflect those changes and fully embrace your new chapter.

As I moved through my set of life changes, it didn't occur to me to check in with my values, but a friend introduced me to her concept of

"What's at your core." About ten years later, as I was receiving training as an Organizing Coach, I realized this concept was similar to some of the coaching activities I was learning about values and needs. It's important to reflect on what you value and to identify what enables you to live a satisfying, fulfilling life with integrity. Identifying your values and needs will be a useful exercise for you as well. Needs are the principles you live by—your personal priorities. Examples of needs are: equality, health, self-worth, spirituality, and peace. You may have some basic needs that were not getting met in your last chapter, so you'll want to start by covering the basics.

Values help you figure out the types of belongings you want in your life, as well as which activities you should devote your time to.

Once your needs are met, you can move on to working on your values to ensure the life you are creating is in alignment with your principles and beliefs. We are happiest when we have a purpose in life and know our values, so take some time with this. Knowing your values will be useful as you begin to change your home to reflect you and your new chapter, as well as change how you use your time. Values help you figure out the types of belongings you want in your life, as well as which activities you should devote your time to, and this can inspire you as you reorganize.

For example, if you want to declutter and reorganize your home, it may be that you want to free up time and space to pursue a dream you've always had, such as writing a book, starting a new business, or creating an art studio. Think of how motivated you'll be if you have a specific reason to start and complete this reorganizing project.

Reorganizing isn't only about moving on and leaving your past behind. Most important, it's about creating a new chapter. You may know just what your new chapter will be like, or you may prefer to let it grow organically, a piece at a time. So do a check on your values as you begin this reorganization process.

Your organizing systems will work best for you and you'll be most motivated to change when you tie organizing to your values. And the systems will persist and support you most effectively if you're clear on what's important to you and design organizing systems that work for you—fitting your style, how you're mentally and emotionally wired, and what you're willing to do to maintain them.

Chapters in books have clear beginnings and endings, and sometimes chapters in life do, too. More often we gradually phase out of one chapter and into another chapter. You may be well into your next chapter before you fully realize it or before you have time to fully adjust to the change. Approaching life in chapters allows you to close the door on the past (while still honoring it) and fully embrace your present. When you live this way, you give yourself permission to let go of things, and you can be more comfortable with choices you make. When you give up something from the past, you'll realize you are not giving up dreams, you're simply making room for them to happen in future chapters. You are not dishonoring memories of those you've loved, but incorporating into your life the most special memories that are the essence of your loved ones.

Life's transitions often require us to reorganize or adapt our current surroundings and schedules. Reorganizing can realign and get us back into balance. The process of reorganizing can point us toward our next new chapter, assisting us before, during and after these major life events. *We regroup, remember, and reorganize—the new Three Rs.*

The goal of this book is to help you find ways to hold on to what's best from your previous chapters, including your belongings, your systems and routines, and how you use your time,

> Reorganizing can realign and get us back into balance. The process of reorganizing can point us toward our next new chapter, assisting us before, during, and after these major life events.

while deciding what you need around you right now, and also what you'll need as you move through this transition into your next chapter of life.

The mental and physical space we create by letting go of things that belong in our past gives us new energy for our next chapter. The space gives us serenity, calm, control, or the option to fill the space with something new. Our focus is forward, with respect for what's behind us—because what's behind us is a large part of who we have become.

Transitions add the twists and turns in this journey of life. They are tough to go through, certainly. But once on the other side of the transition, given time, most of us will feel like we've conquered something truly significant in our lives. And if we can do that, what else can we do? After I experienced all those significant changes in those brief eighteen months, I took a little time to reflect and decided I was ready to listen to my friend Roberta's idea about becoming a professional organizer and starting my own business. Why not? If I had made it through the other changes ... then what else could I do?

"Though no one can go back and make a brand-new start, anyone can start from now and make a brand-new ending."

—AUTHOR UNKNOWN

My goal with this book is to empower you to embrace your changes and not just to weather them, but sail through them so you can find all of the wonderful opportunities on the other side, which is the fresh start you are looking for. I'll share what I've learned and experienced through my own changes, as well as what I've learned and experienced through my clients, my class attendees, and my colleagues. When you're a Certified Organizer Coach® and Certified Professional Organizer®, people like to share with you how they organize their space, stuff, and life! Clients discuss memories, values, and obstacles as their trust in the professional organizer grows.

I am honored and privileged by what people have shared with me over the years, and I would certainly not ever compromise these conversations. The examples I share in this book are composites of my clients and students, and they are not based on any one specific person. I have purposefully mixed up and changed details so no one is recognizable. That said, I'm sure clients and colleagues will think they recognize themselves. If one client's experience is recognizable, that's because there are enough similarities with the next person's experience to make the experiences seem the same. Organizer coaches call this normalizing. The changes you experience aren't all that different from those experienced by someone else in a similar situation. Doesn't it feel so much better when we know we're not alone in this?

DEFINITIONS: TRANSITION VERSUS CHANGE

I want to take a few minutes to compare and contrast transition and change to help you understand why this time in your life can be mentally or emotionally difficult and then relate this difficulty to your organizing dilemmas. Expectations are everything. They make a situation either harder or easier, depending on what we expected going into it.

Change is a Difference

A change is one single difference that happens during one specific event or at one point in time. It's over fairly quickly, and when you compare the before and after, it's black-and-white. In other words, changes are sudden, but they aren't always unexpected. Examples of a change are losing a job, giving birth to a baby, or welcoming a puppy into your home.

Dictionary.com defines *change* this way: "… to make the form, nature, content, future course, etc., of (something) different from what it is or from what it would be if left alone: to change one's name; to change one's opinion; to change the course of history."[1] And the verb is defined as: "to become different."

With a change, you know how things are going to be, and you can begin to adjust to it and reorganize your surroundings as soon as you've mentally and emotionally processed the change (which may take some significant time, depending on the change). After you adjust to the change, your organizing systems should require little to no adjustment if you maintain them.

Transition is a Process

A transition is not so black-and-white. A transition is not a single point in time; it's a shift, like on a spectrum. Transition occurs over a longer period of time than change does. When I think of transitions, it's more about a state of mind or your mind-set. Transition is a gradual series of changes that lead you to a new point in life. Gray instead of black-and-white.

> A transition is not so black-and-white. A transition is not a single point in time; it's a shift, like on a spectrum. Transition occurs over a longer period of time than change does.

Dictionary.com defines *transition* as: "passage ... from one ... state, stage, subject to another."[2] *Passage* is the key word. It's not a door, which is quickly opened and shut, but a passage that you must journey through. You may experience many transitions before a change occurs. For example, if you are preparing to retire, you may transition from working full time to working part time to not working at all. Caregiving often is transition, as you gradually take on more and more responsibility for the person you are caring for. You may start by caregiving in your parent's home once or twice a week. Over time that may increase to visiting every day, and eventually you may have your parent move in with you, or you may help them move to an assisted living facility. You may transition as you change careers by first going back to school for more education.

With transitions, you aren't sure of the final outcome. Everything is temporary, so you may feel like you are in limbo. You can and should create organizing systems to help you through the transition, but these systems won't be permanent. You will need to adjust them frequently as you continue to transition, and after your transition culminates in a change, you will need to reset your organizing systems to support the change. So don't be discouraged if you feel like you just can't get or stay organized during a transition. Do the best you can, and be aware of all the subtle changes that are taking place during the transition. If you identify the change, you can work to accommodate it in your organizing system.

> Don't be discouraged if you feel like you just can't get or stay organized during a transition. Do the best you can.

This book is written to assist you in organizing your life, your stuff, and your home through transitions. Here's just one example of a transition and how organizing can support you.

Identifying Changes and Transitions

Let's look at an example to help you identify transitions and changes in your own situation. Mary is in her sixties, and her mother is in her eighties. Mary's been divorced for a while and living on her own. She's accustomed to having a space of her own and coming and going when she likes. Her mother suddenly falls ill and, like with many families, they decide that Mom will move in with Mary instead of putting Mom in a nursing home. Is this a change or transition?

It's both, but here, thinking of the situation as a transition is key to both Mary's and her mother's mental health. If you thought of this as just a change, with Mom changing homes, then you'd likely think that once she's moved in, the change is over. Life will go back to normal, or to what it was like before Mom moved in, but that's not the case at all.

If Mary realizes that this is a major difference for both her and her mother, she will know that things will change to a *new normal*, a state which both of them need to create together. Mary will need to adjust to having her mother in her home. She will need to create space for her mother in a home that previously only needed to meet Mary's needs. She will need to include her mother in her schedule by making time for her appointments and caring for her needs. She needs to understand that her mother will want to know where she's going and how long she'll be gone when Mary leaves the house. Mary will need to create a bedroom and personal space in her home for her mother and organize the furniture and items her mother is bringing with her. She'll also need to work with her mother and other family members to properly take care of items that won't or can't be moved into Mary's house. There's so much to be done! If Mary approaches it as a transition, she can take things one step at a time. That will help keep her from becoming overwhelmed and frustrated.

> "Much as we may wish to make a new beginning, some part of us resists doing so as though we were making the first step toward disaster."
>
> – WILLIAM BRIDGES

William Bridges, author of *Transitions*, identifies the three parts of a major life transition: an ending, a neutral zone (I call that one "limbo land"), and the new beginning.[3] The length of each phase is different, and they flow into each other. In Mary's example, both Mary and her mother experience the same ending. Both women are losing their independence. Mary is no longer free to come and go as she pleases, and she must make room in her house for her mother. Mary's mother must accept that she can no longer live alone and must rely on her daughter for daily assistance. The neutral zone is the time it takes each woman to adjust to the new living situation. They will start their new beginning together after they've created a schedule that works for each of them and found the right arrangement and balance for their belongings in Mary's home.

As you approach and go through the transition process, you will feel challenged and stressed internally, and perhaps externally, to relinquish what is comfortable and familiar. The familiar is slowly becoming your "old" life or your previous chapter of life. This is a push to let go of your physical stuff, how your schedule was organized, and how you organized your thoughts, your emotions, and your life. Embrace this feeling. Give yourself permission to let go. Use the advice in this book to make what I call "no regret" decisions about letting go of belongings and old routines. The longer you hold on to your old ways, the more resistance builds, and the more stuck you begin to feel. You will feel "unstuck" and less stressed when you let go. Letting go helps you move on and move forward. I've found that it often is highly organized and structured people who have the hardest time with transitions. In an attempt to maintain control, they hold on to their old organizational systems too long. Organizing systems are good things, but they are only effective when they serve you. If you serve your organizing system, it will stress you out and keep you from moving forward. Allow your routines to be flexible and adapt them to meet your needs. Try different approaches to find what works best.

> It often is highly organized and structured people who have the hardest time with transitions. In an attempt to maintain control, they hold on to their old organizational systems too long.

TYPES OF CHANGES AND TRANSITIONS

There are many types of transitions. Understanding what type of transition you are going through will help you know what to expect from the transition—both emotionally and physically.

Self-Imposed or Non-Self-Imposed

Examples of self-imposed transitions are a new career, a separation or divorce you wanted or needed, babysitting grandchildren, or starting a new business. All situations you wanted. Examples of non-self-imposed transitions are a divorce you didn't want, the death of a family member or spouse, a job layoff or termination, a medical diagnosis, and so forth. They are changes and situations that happened to you.

A self-imposed change and transition process can be just as difficult to navigate as a change imposed by other people *even if it's one you sought out*. You may be saying, "I should be happy about this. I caused it. I wanted it." True, but that doesn't mean you don't feel strongly about what's happening. It doesn't mean things aren't changing. Change and the transition process are going to happen, regardless of whether the situation is one you wanted or one that happened to you.

Mary's example could have been a self-imposed situation—she may have wanted her mother to move in with her. But it also could have been something she felt pressured to do by other family members.

One-at-a-Time or Many

Sometimes transitions happen one at a time, and you have time to thoroughly process the event before the next change happens. But often one transition will cause another transition and then another and then another, like a ripple effect. Say, for example, you lost your job, and the loss of income required you to move to a smaller home or apartment, and perhaps go back to school for more training. One event can trigger several changes, or several unrelated changes can happen within a short time frame. When you don't have time to process the first transition, the second transition can be very difficult to deal with.

One client experienced the sudden death of her father, whom she was very close to. She kept as much of his stuff as possible, but simply placed it on top her own stuff in her house. She didn't find homes for the items because she was still focused on the grieving process. Before she had a chance to properly deal with her father's belongings, she was laid off from her corporate career, which had been key to her identity. She was already not in the strongest emotional place, and now she was hit hard by losing her job, her career, and part of her identity. What would she do with herself? What would she do when she woke up each day? She started back to school but couldn't wrap her mind around a new field. Meanwhile, she ignored her home. She'd look around and see her father's things and memories everywhere, even though by this point it had been several years since he died. His belongings were starting to have too strong a hold on her emotions, particularly with the loss of her job. She called me to help her organize her home and make it a calm, more emotionally inviting place.

When you don't deal with the organizing effects of the first transition, the second one creates a new layer of stuff (emotional and physical), and as days go by, it becomes harder and harder to believe you can dig out from all of your clutter and identify what you want and need from what you don't. It's harder to envision your space and how it can be beautiful and homey again. It's harder to see ahead in your life and reorganize your time and activities to move on to your new chapter. You get used to living the old way and not moving on. But eventually something happens and an alarm in your head goes off. You've had enough of the "clutter." You feel suffocated by memories instead of enjoying them. You've reached a point when you can reorganize. Because you are reading this book, you probably have already reached this point, or you are about to reach it very soon. The following chapters will show you how to identify the things you need and love from the clutter so you can move forward.

When you don't deal with the organizing effects of the first transition, the second one creates a new layer of stuff (emotional and physical).

STAGES OF CHANGE

According to the Prochaska Change Model, there are five stages of change: precontemplation, contemplation, preparation, action, and maintenance.[4] I mention this because if you sense where you are on this spectrum, you'll know more about what to expect from yourself.

Precontemplation: You are not yet considering a change.

Contemplation: You're considering a change, such as working on reorganizing your home, but you're not quite ready to dive in. You're still weighing your options.

Preparation: You're thinking about making the change in the next month or so and considering what could be a small first step.

Action: You are making the change. In our case, you're doing the physical work of organizing.

Maintenance: Maintenance is the efforts you make after the change to maintain the results brought about by the change. In our case, after you've reorganized, you maintain by continuing to put things in their established homes, and you work on instilling new organizing habits or skills.

Let's apply these stages to the example of Mary and her mother. The precontemplation stage probably occurred before a decline in the mother's health. Mary's mother was still okay living on her own.

As it became apparent that Mary's mother would not be able to care for herself in her own home for much longer, Mary and her siblings began the contemplation stage. Something needed to change to keep their mother safe, healthy, and well cared for. They considered all of their options, which included a nursing home, an assisted living facility, and living with a family member, and they eventually decided their mother would live with Mary. They also needed to seek input from their mother during this stage.

During the preparation stage, the family decides what furniture and belongings should move to Mary's house; decides what should be done with the rest of their mother's belongings; identifies which room in Mary's house could be used by her mother as a bedroom and personal space; and determines if Mary's home will need any special equipment, ramps, and handrails to make it easier for their mother.

The action phase involves actually implementing all of the decisions Mary and her siblings made in the preparation stage. In this stage Mary rearranges her home to include a bedroom and personal space for her mother, has necessary equipment added to her home, moves her mother's belongings to Mary's house, and distributes the rest of her mother's things according to the decisions made during the preparation stage.

The maintenance stage is the time Mary and her mother spend adjusting their schedules and their surroundings to better accommodate their individual needs and responsibilities.

HOW THIS BOOK CAN ASSIST YOU

As you move from one life chapter to another, your organizational systems can support you through the transitions, if you let them. You'll have an easier time when you recognize that your life is changing and figure out how your systems need to change. You'll feel more in control.

We all deal with change at different rates and in different ways. Some of us love the variety that change brings into our lives. Others want stability—the least amount of change possible. In my experience, the more structured you are, the harder it is to deal with these transitions. These life events are not single-point-in-time changes. They are part of a transition process, a chapter of your life that is ongoing, even if it is brief.

> As you move from one life chapter to another, your organizational systems can support you through the transitions, if you let them.

The event has changed you in some significant way, and you may not know how until you're far on the other side of the change. But at some point, those changes become overwhelming, and you feel like you are in limbo. You can't mentally process the changes any faster. Or you are in a whole new set of circumstances that require you to change how you organize your activities and your home.

This book can help you if you are going through some life transitions right now. It will help you identify which changes, even small but important ones, can help you feel like some part of your life is under control. You'll update and reorganize parts of your life and parts of your home as you process the changes, bit by bit. If you've experienced or are experiencing any of the following transitions, this book will help you set up organizing systems to handle the change and welcome your next chapter in life:

- New energy in your home. This includes the birth of a child, baby-sitting grandchildren, or taking in a new pet. With this transition, you will reorganize to incorporate the new energy and get your life back under control by building a new schedule and surroundings that accommodate the change.

- Postdivorce. Your reorganizing efforts will focus on supporting the new and single you.

- Empty nesting. Now that your home and your time are your own, you can reinvent the functions of your rooms and explore fun and exciting ways to use your time.

- Your partner or spouse died. Reorganizing will honor your past while allowing you to move forward at your own pace.

- Major career change. Perhaps you're changing fields, switching shifts, or moving from a corporate setting to self-employment. You'll need to reorganize your time and your schedule, and set up an office if you work from home.

- Assisting aging parents. You'll need to reorganize your time to incorporate caregiving, deal with their home (whether they are moving out or need a better setup for continued independence), and possibly reorganize your home to accommodate them if they are moving in with you.

- Downsizing. You can reduce the amount of stuff in your home and schedule whether you are moving or staying in place. Owning less can be quite freeing.

- Health diagnosis. Physical issues such as arthritis, fibromyalgia, and other diagnoses may require you to reorganize your home so it is easy for you to maneuver. Your schedule may need to change as well, simply because it takes you longer to move or accomplish a task. Brain-based challenges, such as an adult ADHD diagnosis, necessitate new ways of organizing so life becomes easier again.

This book can also help you if you are overwhelmed by more than one of these life changes. You're coming to the last page of your previous chapter and are getting ready to move on to your next chapter in life. Clients seek me out after they have processed and accepted much of the change in their lives. They are ready to reorganize and start their next life chapter. Often it takes all the energy you have to manage your mental and emotional health during the changes. Your home and organizational systems fall by the wayside. When your emotions are under control and you've mentally processed the change, you realize you need to make up for the neglect your home has suffered, and you need to reorganize your home to better fit your new chapter in life. You need to get back on track, and that's exactly what this book will assist you with.

When your emotions are under control and you've mentally processed the change, you realize you need to make up for the neglect your home has suffered.

The Functions of This Book

Everyone will have different needs as they begin this journey. The book can serve several roles, depending on what you need. Here are just a few ways this book can help:

Educator and coach. I'll provide you with education, suggestions, exercises, and checklists to help you organize in new, effective ways, and I'll also help you realize just how much you do know about your personal organizing methods and styles. When it comes to organizing, what matters most is that the system works for you—there's no right or wrong way to do it. Often you'll find the answers are inside you, not so far away at all; you just don't realize it.

> "Chaos is the primal state of pure energy for every true new beginning."
>
> –WILLIAM BRIDGES & ASSOCIATES, WWW.WMBRIDGES.COM

A quiet but inspirational companion. In reading this book, you'll realize that what you're going through is similar to what many others have gone through before you. This feeling of not being alone is inspiring to many people. The practical suggestions in this book will motivate you to get started, which sometimes is the hardest part of all. Think of this book as a partner to accompany you on your reorganizing journey.

Your personal champion. This book is here to cheer you on and keep you going.

Lifelong friend. My hope is that anytime you realize you're about to go through some significant change, you'll turn to this book and allow it to assist you again.

What does your next chapter hold for you, and what does that mean about your home, your office, your schedule? What does "organized enough" mean to you now? What does the phrase "keeping my schedule under control" mean to you now? What do you want out of your home, your time, and your life? How do you want your house to "talk to you," as one woman explained to me when we started working together? What tone of voice; what words? Or what do you say to yourself? This book will help you find answers to all of these questions.

Let's begin the journey. I'll be alongside you on your journey. You might be ready to make lots of changes, or you might be ready to start small and return to the journey at a later time. I'll be here.

NOTES

1 Dictionary.com, "Change," http://dictionary.reference.com/browse/change (accessed March 9, 2011)

2 Dictionary.com, "Transition," http://dictionary.reference.com/browse/transition (accessed March 9, 2011)

3 William Bridges, *Transitions: Making Sense of Life's Changes, Revised 25th Anniversary Edition* (Cambridge, Massachusetts: Da Capo Press, 2004).

4 James O. Prochaska, John C. Norcross, and Carlo C. DiClemente, *Changing for Good* (New York: Avon Books, 1994).

2. Set Organizing Goals

YOU HAVE DECIDED TO REORGANIZE your home, your belongings, and your schedule. You recognized that something is not working, and you want to change it. Congratulations. That alone is a huge first step. You've also just come through a major life transition (or are going through one right now) and are starting your next life chapter. Another congratulations for starting with a fresh outlook on the rest of your life.

So where to begin? When I work with people, many want to know where we're headed. They want to understand the big picture. To give them a path for this journey, I created two descriptions of the reorganizing process. The difference between the two is the end goal.

The first is called REORGANIZE. It is a practical approach that deals with organizing spaces and belongings. Each letter in the word *reorganize* represents a different step in the organizing process. You can find the steps at the end of the chapter. Read this one and see if it resonates with you.

The other is called SIMPLIFY. It is more holistic in its view and focuses on your approach more than the actual steps. This process can be applied to anything you want to simplify, whether it's your belongings, your schedule, or your organizing systems. Read the details of this system at the end of this chapter.

This chapter focuses on the *S* in SIMPLIFY, which stands for "set the stage" and the *R* in REORGANIZE, which stands for "ready"—readiness for change. Because you've purchased this book, you must be considering reorganizing and/or simplifying, so that's your first step. You'll want to reflect a bit on where you're headed, whether you can imagine the entire new picture or just its first step. Neither method is right or wrong. Whatever fits for you is what's right. You'll also reflect on your past as it relates to organization. Some people will find their reorganization will mostly be about moving on from their pasts without knowing much about where they're headed. Others may be able to envision their next chapter, or they may be well into it.

> Some people will find their reorganization will mostly be about moving on from their pasts without knowing much about where they're headed. Others may be able to envision their next chapter, or they may be well into it.

As we begin to reorganize, you must realize that for your new systems to truly support you, you need to evaluate your needs and goals for this next chapter in life. When you know what you want and where you are going, you can identify the tools you need and position them to best help you. If you skip this part and simply start purging and rearranging your belongings, you may find you've done nothing more than clean house, and the clutter will return very quickly. You also may find you get rid of either too much stuff or not enough stuff.

It's difficult, but worth it, to use some of your precious mental energy to figure out how to adapt your systems. Most of your mental energy goes toward surviving the transition itself, but if you can slow down and focus on making some adjustments to your organizing systems, the transition actually goes more smoothly, because with organizing systems to support you, you get control over the basics of daily life. The systems keep you from worrying about the small stuff in life, which only adds to your energy drain. I've seen this principle proven time and time again with my clients and in my own life.

Let's briefly look at this transition you've been through or are going through so you can begin to think about how the transition will affect your surroundings. Reflect a bit before launching into an organizing project so you know where you're headed.

> "When one door closes, another opens; but we often look so long and so regretfully upon the closed door that we do not see the one which has opened for us."
>
> —ALEXANDER GRAHAM BELL

Who are you becoming? What is this new chapter going to be about—and therefore, which of your belongings will you carry forward? Surrounding yourself with things that support your move forward, rather than drag you down or keep you in the past, is key.

You may want to get some extra support or an outsider's perspective to move you through this process of beginning your next chapter. Some of you will want additional support related to your past, to work through emotions, gain perspective, and move on. Others are already looking forward and need an expert guide or coach to move on.

It's often difficult to reflect on your own. If you get stuck, use some of these prompts:

- *See a life coach or a therapist.* What's the essential difference? Life coaches look forward to help you create your future. Therapists help you review the past and gain perspective; they help with emotional obstacles.
- *Journal* on the topic of your next chapter.
- *Create a vision board.* Find photos and phrases that help describe where you are headed and what you want from your next chapter. A vision board is useful because you can post it where you can see

it every day. Plus the process of thinking about what belongs on your board is as useful as the results.

- *Use a series of affirmations.* These have helped some of my clients.
- *Go on meditative retreats,* silent or not. Take a day (or week!) away for yourself.
- *Read books.* I loved *Simple Abundance* by Sarah Ban Breathnach and *What's Next* by Rena Pederson when I needed to create my next chapter.

You can start organizing as you try these ideas. Sometimes we know much more than we think we do. You may be all set to move ahead by answering the questions in the next few pages. I know that it can be unnerving not to have all the answers, to feel like you're in limbo, to berate yourself (some of you will do this) for not knowing enough right now. The exciting thing is that you're starting a new chapter of your life. You don't know all the details, but you get to paint the picture yourself.

Use the following exercise to help you identify your organizing goals before you start organizing. Take your time to answer the questions as thoughtfully and honestly as possible. Don't worry if you get stuck on some of them. Typically, one or two questions resonate with each individual I work with. If you get stuck, take some time. Go away for a bit and come back later. Setting goals will make your organizing efforts more efficient, more productive, and longer lasting because they will fit your new lifestyle and meet your needs.

> Setting goals will make your organizing efforts more efficient, more productive, and longer lasting because they will fit your new lifestyle and meet your needs.

Create a Vision for Your Organizing Efforts

1. Complete this phrase: My _____ (house, schedule, closet, etc.) is organized enough when …

There are a few ways to reflect on this question. You could choose a current room system that feels organized or reflect on a past system or room in a previous home that felt organized. Why do you feel it is organized? Describe it here. How does it look? Feel? What's it about, this sense of a room being organized enough? There are no right or wrong answers. What matters is that it works for you.

Another approach is to imagine the room you're sitting in were organized enough for you to be pleased with the results. What could you do in here that you can't do now? If my _____

_____room

(living room, bedroom, etc.) were organized enough, I'd be able to

_____

_____

_____

_____.

2. What do you know about what you want for your house, your belongings, your schedule, and your life in general?

3. What do you value most about yourself, your relationships, and the nature of your work? Name your current values, needs, and priorities. If we can connect your organizing goal to one of these, it will be easier for you to stay on track with your organizing, to get motivated, and to sustain!

4. What organizing system do you feel most proud of? What organizing system, at any time in your life, has worked for you? Describe it, thinking about why it worked. What worked about it for you?

5. Was there a time in your life when you felt as organized as you now want to be? If so, what was different then? What worked? What didn't work? What really resonated for you?

6. What has worked well in the past?

7. What have you tried so far?

8. How do you talk to yourself about your home and its organization? Or how does your home talk to you (how does it make you feel)?

9. Do you have issues with staying focused or becoming easily distracted? If so, how does this affect your organizational abilities, your home, and your time? How does it show up in your life?

10. What gets in the way of your home being as organized as you'd like it to be?

11. How does not being as organized as you would like impact your life?

12. When your home is organized the way you'd like it to be, how will things be easier? How will it feel or look? What will you say to friends? (This is sometimes a difficult one until after we've started organizing. Sometimes it's hard to see through to the new picture.)

13. What immediate change would make the biggest impact to your current situation?

Reorganizing is often a great time to process what's going on. It's cathartic, like running, swimming, or mediating. Rearranging your belongings and changing up your space is often an outer reflection of what is going on inside.

As you reorganize your home, you will be amazed at how much thinking you'll do. Reorganizing is often a great time to process what's going on. It's cathartic, like running, swimming, or meditating. Rearranging your belongings and changing up your space is often an outer reflection of what is going on inside. The more you focus on organizing, the more you learn about what you want for your next chapter. You'll have more answers as your mind-set shifts and you move through the transition. Here are examples of people who reorganized their homes as they were exploring the next chapter of their lives.

When Kathryn and I worked together, she had one foot in the previous chapter of her life and a toe dipped into her next chapter. She contacted me a few years after her husband died in his late forties. She still lived in the home they'd bought together only a couple of years before

The more you focus on organizing, the more you learn about what you want for your next chapter.

he died. She still worked at the same company and attended the same church they'd been active in together. She'd made some new friends, somewhat reluctantly. She was not through processing her grief, but she had moved beyond the early stages enough to realize she needed and wanted to make her own life. She had done some initial simplifying in response to her transition by finding some wonderful new homes for her husband's closet full of clothing. When she contacted me, her goal was to let go of more of her husband's things, change the energy in her home, and begin moving forward to create her new chapter. Together, we came up with several specific organizing goals including the following:

- Going over his memorabilia and reducing the amount she kept
- Going through the boxes in the garage that were never opened when they had moved into their new home
- Going through his clothing that was stored in a secondary closet
- Going through his books
- Finding a home for anything new that we brought into her home and creating systems if necessary
- Using her own items to reorganize any space we opened up by reducing his presence in her home

Did Kathryn know exactly who she was becoming when she started organizing? Not necessarily, but here is what she did know: She knew she was becoming a woman who owned a home by herself. She needed to take over responsibility for the chores and organizational systems her husband used to take care of. She was becoming a single woman in her social life. Upon the advice of a good friend, she had decided she would not make a change in her work life for at least a year. She knew she could count on her family. They'd been there for her and would continue to be there for her, no matter what changed in her life. She had developed some new friends at work. She was carving out her own role at her church and in that community.

So Kathryn actually knew a lot when she discussed her next chapter with me. And that knowledge was a great starting point. Over the next few years, she would continue to branch out on her own, changing work, changing church communities, developing new hobbies, changing her diet, and getting to the gym. It's often true that when you have one major change in your life, others eventually follow. Or as one woman said to me, "If I can make it through that change so well, what else can I do? A lot!"

> It's often true that when you have one major change in your life, others eventually follow. Or as one woman said to me, "If I can make it through that change so well, what else can I do? A lot!"

Sandra was in a similar situation in that she was beginning to consider options for her next chapter. She had built a successful business on her own before she got married. The work was physical, and shortly after she got married, she had a significant medical issue that prevented her from doing her work. She saw various medical and holistic professionals and learned there would be no cure for her. She had to figure out for herself how to give up the work she loved and create something new.

Sandra called me after she had sold her business. She was doing pretty well accepting that she'd have to discover a new passion to turn into work for herself. She was considering several avenues. So as she was breaking away from the previous chapter of her life (her years as a business owner) and beginning to build the new, she discovered a need to also shed old belongings from her home. She and her husband hadn't lived in their house very long, so the old belongings were mainly things brought from their last home but never unpacked at their new home.

So our reorganizing goals included the following:

- Sort through the unpacked boxes and decide what stayed or went.
- Find homes for items that stayed.
- Find places to donate items she didn't want to keep.
- Create an exercise space that would help her manage her medical condition.
- Create an office space where she could start seriously working on her new business ideas.
- Simplify in general. She wanted to get control over pockets of clutter, including papers in the kitchen, excess bathroom products, and closets that contained clothing no longer worn.

You don't need to know exactly where you're headed to begin figuring out what will come with you to your exciting next chapter.

Sandra was moving on and making changes in many aspects of her life. She didn't know what the next chapter held, but she was turning the last pages of the current chapter, and she was ready to make decisions about what to bring forward with her.

One last story about moving ahead without the complete picture. I coached a woman who owned her own business. She was concerned and anxious about not knowing where her life was headed. In her mind, everyone else seemed to have visions of where they wanted to be in five or ten years. She didn't have this vision, and so she felt lost.

As we coached together, she had a key insight about herself: By nature, she is creative. Locking herself into a five-year plan felt very uncreative to her. She realized that organically creating her next chapter would work better for her. After she realized this, I could hear her voice relax without the pressure of what "everyone else" was doing, and then she was able to get organized to begin creating her next chapter.

As these examples show, you don't need to know exactly where you're headed to begin figuring out what will come with you to your exciting next chapter. You can make a good start at simplifying and re-organizing, which will change the look, the feel, and the energy in your home—all of which will be a part of what will propel you forward to living your next chapter.

Reorganize Your Surroundings

R   **READY.** Are you ready to reorganize? Are you ready to change habits to make this work? What happens if you don't move ahead? What's motivating you? Why now and not before now? (See chapter two.)

E   **EVALUATE.** What do you like about this room or other rooms that are a model for what you want? What's working? Not working? If you have tried to reorganize your space or your schedule in the past, what worked or didn't work? (See chapter five.)

O   **OBJECTIVES.** What do you want to do that you can't? How do you want the space or your schedule to feel, look, be? Decide on the purpose for your space. (See chapter five.)

R   **ROUND AND ROUND.** Make up your boxes. Take out everything that doesn't belong, even if you don't know where it will go. You have to start somewhere! Stay in the room you're working on; it will be tempting to reorganize the space you move things to. (See chapter six.)

G   **GET RID OF (OR NOT?).** Decisions, decisions. Use the no-regrets questions list (see page 101). (See chapter six.)

A   **ANALYZE REMAINING ITEMS.** Think areas or sections of activities. Organize by area instead of looking at the space as a whole. Organize belongings by how often you use them. Keep the daily use items within easy reach. Keep the occasionally used nearby, but not in your everyday space. Keep I-use-it-a-few-times-a-year items out of sight—in a closet or in another room. (See chapter seven.)

N   **NEGOTIATE THE SPACE VERSUS YOUR BELONGINGS.** Measure and count the items you're going to containerize. Also measure the space the container needs to fit into. Go vertical and use the walls. On shelves, use containers. Use drawer organizers to keep items together. (See chapter seven.)

I   **IMPLEMENT.** Implement your ideas in each area, one section at a time. Don't try to reorganize the whole room at once. Move furniture around. See which layout makes you feel productive or inspired or comfortable. Find or buy new storage containers and put the room back together. (See chapter seven.)

Z   **ZEBRA!** Be one. Each zebra has a unique set of stripes. So do we. Your organizing solutions are unique to how you live and work. Give yourself a chance to try new space, skills, and/or habits. (See chapter seven.)

E   **EVALUATE, EVALUATE.** Each piece of paper creates a pile. Each new item of clothing makes the others more wrinkled. Always be thinking as you look around—am I satisfied with how this works? If you go through a major life event, evaluate how you're organizing for it. What works for you in one stage will need to change as you move on to another stage. (See chapter seven.)

Simplify Your Life

(S) **SET THE STAGE.** Are you ready for change? What's the easiest way for you to start? What happens if you don't move ahead? What's motivating you? What do you like? Dislike? What's working? Not working? What frustrates you? What do you like about other, more organized spaces? (See chapter two.)

(I) **INVOLVE OTHERS.** Who might enjoy belongings you think you'll give away? Who could work with you on boxing up things? Who can take away things you no longer want? Who can help you make good decisions? (See chapter four.)

(M) **MAKE SMALL STEPS.** Break down your project into the smallest of steps, until you look at what you've written and think, "That's easy enough. I can do that." Or focus on an amount of time you know you can work with. (See chapters four and five.)

(P) **PLAN TO CONTINUE.** Plan a regular time of day, a regular day of the week, or use vacation time. Focus on moving around the room like clockwork so you can quickly see your progress. Go around and around until you finish the space; don't leave it while you're working, or you may end up reorganizing another space you hadn't intended to. (See chapter four.)

(L) **LET GO WITHOUT REGRETS.** Ask yourself enough questions about each item so you don't end up regretting any decisions. If you need to set aside a few items to put on probation or decide on later, put them in a box and mark a date: "Decide by … " (e.g., three months from today's date). (See chapter six.)

(I) **IMPLEMENT YOUR IDEAS.** It's a new chapter, try new ideas. Try out your ideas and give them some time to work. Changes (like new organizing systems) take twenty-one times in use to become a habit, longer if you have ADHD or other brain-based challenges. Have patience with yourself; this is a lot of change at once. (See chapters six and seven.)

(F) **FINE-TUNE YOUR IDEAS.** Take stock. What's working well? Pat yourself on the back. What's not working the way you intended? Pat yourself on the back for trying; reality sometimes changes our best laid plans. So let's change the plans then. (See chapter seven.)

(Y) **YOU DID IT.** Congratulations! Now … where to next?

3. Establish and Evaluate Organizing Systems— The Three Ps

WHEN YOU THINK ABOUT ORGANIZING OR REORGANIZING, there's a simple phrase that will help you determine what is not working with your organizing systems: people, process, products—the Three Ps.

People are the individuals who use or impact the system, and it includes their mind-set and habits.

Process is the step-by-step actions the people take to implement and maintain the system.

Products are the containers, items, or furniture needed to support the system. The products need to work well for the person and the process.

An effective organizing system is made up of all three of these elements. If one element is not working for you, the system will not give you the results you want. If all three elements are not working, it's only a matter of time before you will need to overhaul your room or home again because the clutter will return. The Three Ps require a bit of forethought. Don't just think about the organizing makeover you're about to launch. Think ahead a bit, too, to what kind of maintenance your organizing system will require. Sometimes the system seems perfect until you realize how complicated it's going to be to keep up with it. It may take too many steps, require too much time, or be theoretically perfect but

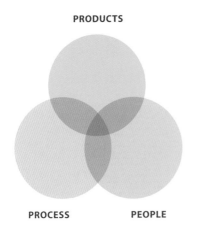

PRODUCTS

PROCESS   **PEOPLE**

not practical. If you can't look ahead to the maintenance on your own, then you may want to talk it through with a Certified Organizer Coach®. You can certainly also ask friends and family how they handle their own organizing system for the same area in their home. You'll get a variety of ideas, and then the challenge will be to figure out which ideas, or mixture of ideas, will work for you and your situation. An organizer coach can assist you with this kind of questioning and reflection. We are experienced not only with implementing various systems, but, more important, with understanding how to assist you in determining what will work for you. Let's look more closely at each of these Three Ps.

People

Early in my career as a professional organizer, I worked with a writer who taught me a crucial lesson about organizing. It's not only about the process or the products; it's about the people, our habits, how we are wired, and what we say about our stuff. I've fine-tuned the Three Ps over the years, but this client inspired me to coin the phrase.

Don't just think about the organizing makeover you're about to launch. Think ahead a bit, too, to what kind of maintenance your organizing system will require.

I'll never forget this client, partly because of the person she was, and also because of our discussions on organizing. She considered herself a "naturally unorganized person," and asked how I could help her maintain the organizing systems we put in place in her home office. Making over her office by cleaning out the stuff that didn't belong there felt great. Rearranging the layout improved the creative energy in the room, energy necessary for her writing. The before and after photos looked great, but she worried how she would keep it up without me there. This was the first time I realized staying organized is not only about the products or the process. The key to staying organized starts with the person doing the organizing. What will work for you will not necessarily work for your friend or your sister-in-law. How people maintain organizing systems is personal. How much "stuff" a person can tolerate is also a personal choice.

My organizing systems need to change as my life changes to reflect my new chapter in life. Remember the Three Ps: People, Process, Products.

One thing you don't want to do is compare your home to anyone else's when you begin thinking of organizing goals. Only you and your household get to be the judges of what is organized enough in your home. If you try to organize to someone else's standards, you're not really doing this for yourself. You won't be as engaged or as committed, and the systems will be harder to keep up with because they were not designed for you. Remember, it's all about you!

You must decide for yourself what you want your home and your schedule to look like. Your home does not need to be stark and worthy of a magazine cover to be organized. If you are not a highly structured person, don't aim for perfection. Set loose boundaries that you can easily follow. You will feel better about successfully using a simple system than you will about struggling to obtain perfection.

Organization coaching supports the people aspect because it lets the client devise her own systems and determine maintenance needs, with the help of insightful questions from an organizer coach. You'll find some coaching questions in various sections of this book to help you create and maintain your own individual systems. You can still use the Three Ps on your own, as I'll show you ways you can self-coach.

Remember that the most important element in your organizing system is you. Create a system that you enjoy using—even if it is unlike any system you've ever seen. Organizing is not about "keeping up with the Joneses." It's about helping you use your time and energy efficiently, no matter how that looks. Find what works for you. Do you process things internally, verbally, visually? Think about how you prefer to solve problems and apply these preferences to your organizing systems.

One client uses a tape recorder as she drives in the car. She processes out loud (verbal/speaking modality)[1] most often. She finds that talking out problems, sounding out ideas, and even crafting her written materials is far easier this way. By getting it out of her head and hearing herself speak it aloud, she can think more clearly and problem-solve more effectively.

Another client is strong on the emotional modality. So we know when we sort through a room together, the stories and the sentiment are not just nice to hear but are necessary to her decisions on what to let go of and what to keep. If we didn't realize this, we might cut short the stories or try to discuss only the big ones. But she wouldn't be able to make good decisions, no-regret decisions, if we did that.

> Remember that the most important element in your organizing system is you. Create a system that you enjoy using—even if it is unlike any system you've ever seen.

If your dominant processing modality is auditory, use this to help you remember routines and appointments. Some people focus better when they have an auditory reminder, versus remembering to look at the clock. One woman is introducing morning and evening routines not only to her family, but also to structure her day. She is using her PDA as the timer/reminder, whether it's to remind her to move the laundry to the dryer or to pick up her mother for a doctor's appointment. The auditory reminder works for her, but it may not work for everyone. Some people get so focused on what they are doing they don't hear the alarm. It's not the best way to get their attention.

Process

Once you've identified your organizing preferences and tendencies, you can develop a specific process for your system. This is how you actually use your system. You may compare it to a routine or a habit. It's important to try out your new organizing system long enough to tweak it—or realize this system fits you just right. There's an adage that a habit takes twenty-one days to solidify. I modify this and say organizing systems take twenty-one *times*; some of our organizing systems (like doing laundry or getting to the gym) are not used daily, but the twenty-one times guideline is still pretty accurate. It may take people with ADHD five to seven times longer to make the system a habit. So as you can tell, the length of time is all about you.

As an example, let's look at the organizing system I use to keep track of my keys, PDA, and pocketbook. My process is as follows:

☐ Arrive home and go up the stairs to the front hall closet.

☐ Put the keys on the key holder (currently a glorified old nail, but it works).

☐ My pocketbook goes on the right-hand side of the top shelf of the closet. I've designated the left side of the shelf as my "grab-and-go" section where I place things that I need to take out of the house (a book I borrowed, an item to share with friends, an item I need to return to a store along with its receipt).

☐ I take off my coat, but I keep my PDA in my hand.

☐ I walk around the corner into my home office. I plug in the PDA along with my earpiece.

☐ I place both in their beautiful (and useful) black leather holder, which has six large compartments.

I use these same motions every time I arrive at home. This is my process (which takes less than five minutes), and it helps me immediately put away all of my important items so I always know exactly where they are. There are a lot better ways I can use my time than running around looking for things.

As the Venn diagram on page 47 shows, the process needs to fit the people using it to be truly effective. In the example I just shared, I'm organizing my personal belongings, so I am the only person in this system. I need the system to fit my style, so what do I know about myself? Well, I know that if I put the PDA and earpiece down just anywhere as I take off my coat and put away my pocketbook, I'll forget about them. Someone will ask me a question as I enter the house or my dogs will need a hug or I'll start thinking about something else and not pay attention to what I'm doing. Then I'll forget to put them where they belong, and that means I'll have to run around the house looking for them the next time I need to leave. And worse, because I was distracted at the time, retracing my steps may be literally impossible. So these items stay in my hands until they land in their homes because I know how I'm wired—I know if I'm distracted I will forget.

> As the Venn diagram on page 47 shows, the process needs to fit the people using it to be truly effective.

Products

Products are what you need to complete your organizing system. The term "product" doesn't mean you need to purchase something new or fill your house with organizing gadgets and containers. Anything can be used as a product to support your organizing system.

Let's go back to the example of how I keep track of my keys, PDA, and pocketbook, and identify all of the products I use in the system. In this example they are the shelf in the closet, the key holder (which is just a nail), the PDA charger, and the black leather holder. I could simply put my items on the desk, but putting them in a specific place on the desk lets me know exactly where they are (thus saving me time) and protects them (thus saving me money). The earpiece is so small that it would get lost on my desk, knocked off the desk, or chomped on by a dog should it fall to the floor. If you think it sounds like experience talking, it certainly is!

The term "product" doesn't mean you need to purchase something new or fill your house with organizing gadgets and containers. Anything can be used as a product to support your organizing system.

Although you can use anything you have on hand, use items that you enjoy. You will take more pleasure in using your system and be more motivated if you feel good about all of the elements. For example, I like having brightly colored items in my office, so my bulletin board is covered with bright fabric. The walls are lilac. Even the sticky notes are bright colors. My charger, with its sleek black leather and six compartments, has a different look and feel from the rest of the room, and this motivates me to use it.

It's important to understand how these Three Ps work together before you begin tackling an organizing project, whether it's a system, an entire room, a paper pile, your laundry process, or your schedule. The Three Ps will help you figure out where the real issue or problem is and will show you what is already working very well about your room/system/time. Sometimes it's so easy to say that the whole room or system isn't working, but really, it's that the storage isn't quite right or we haven't accounted for a new purpose to the room or sometimes, yes, it's that the habits aren't there. So use the Three Ps as your diagnosis tool to recognize what is already working and what needs some life breathed into it. When you use the Three Ps framework for your organizing challenges, you'll gain serenity. You'll save energy, which you need to move through this transition.

Evaluating Your Systems Using the Three Ps

You might be thinking, *but I do all this and my system isn't working for me*, or *I've always done that and I just lost something*. If you are struggling with your old organizing systems that worked for you in the past, I'd bet you are experiencing, or have experienced, a significant change or transition in your life.

Systems have to change as your life changes. By necessity, you probably don't have the exact same schedule every day. Different days have different obligations, and you adjust accordingly. When you are in the midst of a transition, it's necessary for your systems to go with the new flow.

Looking back at my example, how could various life transitions require my organizing system to change?

> "Systems allow ordinary people to achieve extraordinary results, predictably."
>
> —MICHAEL E. GERBER, WWW.E-MYTH.COM

- A parent could move into my house. In that case we would need room on the closet shelf for two pocketbooks.
- My housemate might decide to go into business or is allowed to work from home for the corporation. The office would need to be rearranged, and a second desk would need to be added.
- If I had a child or, at my age, decided to regularly babysit for grandchildren, I would have to change my system because my hands would be full as I entered my house. I would also need to make sure little hands couldn't access these items.

- A physical change such as a disability, shoulder surgery, or age could take place, making it difficult to reach that high shelf. I would need to find a new place for my pocketbook or even find space on the first floor of my home if stairs were an issue.
- We could move to a new home. In that case, all systems would need to be redesigned or created for a new space.

Exercise

I'd like you to give it a try now. Identify one organizing system in your life that needs to support you better than it currently is. If you don't have a structured system in place, simply think of how you currently handle the situation; the actions you currently take are your process (even if they aren't intentional), and the objects you use are your products. Write your answers on a separate sheet of paper.

1. What organizing system is not working well or failing you or doesn't exist yet? If you have trouble with this question, ask yourself what's important to you and just isn't working how you want it to? What used to be so easy and now it's just too hard? What's frustrating?

2. How do you want the system you identified in question 1 to work, to be, to feel, or to look? I ask this question in various ways because for some of us, the energy is important. For others, it's about creating a visual picture of how you want things to look and work for you.

Let's take the Three Ps and apply each one to your challenge. Here's how:

When you are in the midst of a transition, it's necessary for your systems to go with the new flow.

3. Process. To start, identify the process. You can draw it (if it's the layout of a room or closet, for example) or list the steps on index cards, your computer, or sticky notes.

Write one step per card as they come into your head. After all of the ideas are written, you can rearrange them into a specific order. It's amazing how much you learn when you list the steps you need to take.

4. People. Step back. Look at or read your process. Does it look complicated? If so, how can you simplify it? Simple means easier to follow consistently and less maintenance. Because you're in transition, you'll want to keep systems simple so you can focus your attention on the transition itself. Often, I find that when someone has a very structured system that was successful in the past, the system becomes ineffective during a life transition because life has become complicated, and there's just no time to follow what is now a complicated organizing system. If this is your situation, let go of your old system. What's the least amount of process you can get away with, even if it's temporary, while you move through this transition? What can you let go of, do differently, or get assistance for?

> Simple means easier to follow consistently and less maintenance. Because you're in transition, you'll want to keep systems simple so you can focus your attention on the transition itself.

5. People. Identify and list any habits you are going to need to change or establish to get your system in place and maintain it easily. The last items on the list will be habits other people you live with need to change. You'll want to first deal with your own organizing challenges or needs. Show yourself to be the model—and then work with others.

6. People. Now, think of a habit you currently have—something you barely think about, it's so habitual. It could be doing the laundry, being on time, dealing with mail or bills. How did that habit

become so ingrained in you? If you can remember what's worked in the past for you, this may likely work again. Our wiring doesn't change so much that what worked before won't work again. So let's start with a past success. So now, how can you apply what you know about yourself in this past success to the system at hand?

7. Product. List all the physical items your system will need. You don't have to run out and buy these new. Use what you already have around the house. Choose products last, when you know what's needed and where. If you need new shelving, drawer dividers, or containers, measure where you will be using them so you buy products that fit your space. Remember to use items that you enjoy whenever possible.

If you can remember what's worked in the past for you, this may likely work again. Our wiring doesn't change so much that what worked before won't work again. So let's start with a past success.

This evaluation can be used for any room, system, or schedule. Whenever you evaluate a system, start with this exercise.

Use the Three Ps to evaluate every organizing project you undertake. You'll find that the Three Ps will be useful not only as you reorganize your surroundings, but also as you reorganize your schedule and time. We cover managing your time in part three and in part four, we cover staying organized. Come back to this chapter as needed as you work through the rest of this book.

NOTES

1   The first time I heard about processing modalities was during my Coach Approach training, which ultimately led to my Certified Organizer Coach® credential.

Each of us receives, remembers, interprets, uses, and expresses information and activities through processing modalities. Each processing modality is based on specific parts of the body and specialized areas of the brain. There are nine modalities: visual, auditory, kinesthetic, tactile, verbal, emotional, cognitive, intuitive, and taste and smell. Each represents a different kind of information and different way of perceiving information. This Processing Modalities Model was developed by Denslow Brown. It focuses specifically on how people operate through their day—how they get ready for work, run their errands, read their mail, live in their home, function in their workplace, complete daily tasks, and make decisions.

4. Finding Time and Staying Motivated

SOME PEOPLE HAVE TROUBLE GETTING STARTED. Others have trouble sticking with a goal. And still others have difficulty finishing up. This chapter will show you how to make time to organize, motivate you to start organizing, and help you finish strong. We'll cover the *I* (involve others), more of the *M* (make small steps), *P* (plan to continue), and dip into *L* (let go without regrets) from the SIMPLIFY acronym in chapter two.

CREATING TIME FOR REORGANIZING

You may have great intentions to reorganize, but if you don't make time to do the work, your intentions will never translate into actions. Here are a few different approaches to making time to organize. You can get started using one approach and switch to a different approach as needed if your life situation changes. When you break down your organizing plans into specific measurements of time, whether it is a number of minutes per day, a number of days per week, or simply one marathon afternoon per month, you are making small steps toward your organizing goal. That's the *M* in SIMPLIFY. When you make a regular commitment to these steps on your calendar, you are planning how you will continue to organize until you reach your goals. This is the *P* in SIMPLIFY.

Choose the Same Time Daily

This approach makes reorganizing a habit, like drinking your tea or coffee, going to the gym, or meditating. This approach takes away the decision; you just do it automatically after a while. And when I say "daily," I mean on a regular schedule. Your goal might be reorganizing just three times a week, a schedule you know you can easily maintain.

If you choose this schedule, you may want to use the "thirty-minute" approach so you can still carry on with your other obligations and don't get bogged down in the organizing. Whenever you start organizing, set a timer for thirty minutes, or whatever short time period is comfortable to you, and work until the timer goes off. The idea here is simply to get yourself started so you can feel and see the difference in just a short period of time. Some people use a certain number of songs as their "timer." They turn on the radio or recorded music and work through their preset number of songs. You could do the same with a book recording, working through a chapter on the recording. The extra benefit here is that you might just reorganize a little longer because you love the book or the music so much that you don't want to stop!

> You may have great intentions to reorganize, but if you don't make time to do the work, your intentions will never translate into actions.

Customize Each Week on Your Calendar

Sit down each Sunday and decide when you can work on reorganizing this week. The nice part about this approach is that it makes reorganizing easier when your schedule is inconsistent, busy, or involves a fair amount of travel or if you have a varied work schedule. The key here is to write it down on your calendar so you make the commitment on paper, not just in your head. The next page has two examples of how you might identify and designate time to organize if you have a varied schedule. Adding

Examples of Customized Weeks

MONDAY	TUESDAY	WEDNESDAY	THURSDAY
Take care of household & downsizing	1/2 day work	My day out	Volunteer

MONDAY	TUESDAY	WEDNESDAY	THURSDAY
Accounting day—files, CPA meeting, goals	Arts—Photo albums for kids	Lunch appointment; volunteer in the p.m.	Babysit

structure to your week can help you pin down which day could be downsizing day or which part of the day would work best for you.

Use the Blitz Approach
This is when you devote a large block of time to reorganizing. It could be one day each month, such as a Saturday, for example. You'll make a commitment and keep it. And then you only have to worry about reorganizing this one time monthly, not every day or every week. The downside is that projects can take longer, but if you have no particular time frame in mind to be finished, this is a fine option. The upside is that you focus for a dedicated period of time and get a lot accomplished at once. One woman and her husband decided to work on their downsizing projects on various Saturdays after they came back from breakfast with friends. This became a habit, something they barely thought about, so the downsizing didn't take over their lives.

Decide on a Monthly Theme
To keep yourself going, make up a calendar chart so you work on just one room or space each month. You have the entire month to make that space your own, reorganized, and potentially with a new purpose. The monthly theme is a way to break down the entire house into manageable

FRIDAY	SATURDAY	SUNDAY
1/2 day work	Take care of household & downsizing	Take care of household & downsizing

FRIDAY	SATURDAY	SUNDAY
Babysit a.m.; downsizing in the p.m.	Work around the house; landscaping	Church, choir, auction committee

projects and keep you focused on completing one space at a time.

Many people tell me that when they start reorganizing, they move all around the house, attacking this room and then moving on to the next before they fully finish the first. They keep going from room to room without fully finishing. Eventually they get frustrated and give up. A theme can help you stay focused and help you finish strong. If you don't finish a room in a month, carry that room over to the next month. Don't start a new project until you finish your current project.

OVERCOME PROCRASTINATION

Often, scheduling time to organize on your calendar is all you need to do to prompt yourself to start.

Once something works for you, it's worth repeating. We often try to find a new way when we really don't need to; go with what has worked in the past. If that doesn't work, seek out new ways by talking with friends, coaches, colleagues, and family.

But there are times when you might be tempted to procrastinate on your organizing project. As I go through this list of reasons why we procrastinate, think about a time recently when you *knew* you'd procrastinated on a project. *Why* did you? And most important, how did you get yourself started? Try that approach again. Once something works for you, it's worth repeating. We often try to find a new way when we really don't need to; go with what has worked in the past. If that doesn't work, seek out new ways by talking with friends, coaches, colleagues, and family.

Keep breaking down that big project into smaller and smaller steps until you find a step that makes you say, "I can do that." Then take things one step at a time and acknowledge that you are making real progress every time you complete a step, even if it's small.

Here are some ideas for overcoming the common excuses if you're stuck and can't get started again.

It's boring: Make it more interesting by inviting a friend, working in short spurts, or alternating a fun organizing activity (going through memories) with the boring one (going through papers).

Financial worries: Work first on getting key items appraised, or look them up online to get a sense of what you could gain financially if you sold some items. Also understand that you don't need to buy new shelving units, fancy containers, or new décor to organize a room. Work with what you have and remember your goal is to get rid of stuff, not acquire new things.

Lack of goal or deadline: Create a deadline. See page 67 for specific ways to effectively manufacture a deadline.

Past failure experience: Perhaps you tried to get organized in the past and didn't have much success. A lot has changed since your last experience simply because you decided to seek out expertise and bought this book. Keep it by your side. You can do this; you have an expert right here in your hands. Just because you tried something before and it wasn't as successful as you wanted doesn't mean you can't try it again. And, this time, you are probably more ready than you were before to make changes.

Not knowing where to start: Remember the *M* in SIMPLIFY—make small steps. Keep breaking down that big project into smaller and smaller steps until you find a step that makes you say, "I can do that." Then take things one step at a time and acknowledge that you are making real progress every time you complete a step, even if it's small.

Fear of making the wrong decision: Sometimes we feel overwhelmed because we put pressure on ourselves to make the first attempt be the only attempt. We want the first attempt to be our best, perfect solution. And we sometimes think that if we can't do our best, why bother to start? So we don't and things stay the same.

To get past this fear, change your language. Give yourself permission to say, "This is a rough, rough draft," or it is the "first attempt of many," or "I'm just going to take a crack at it." And then believe it. Gradual results over time are just as valid, and often easier to maintain, than a sweeping change. So if your ultimate goal is to give your daughter a redecorated room, but you haven't found the right furniture yet, think temporary. What can you do for her now so she can enjoy her uncluttered room? Do that thing, and think of this as temporary, a rough draft, a first attempt—with much more to come later. Keep track of your ideas for the future in a notebook so you don't lose all that creative thinking.

Consult chapter six for a list of questions that will help you make no-regrets decisions. Ask yourself these questions as you are deciding whether to keep an item. They will help you make a decision that you can feel good about. You can also give yourself permission to delay a decision, which will take some of the pressure off. Put the item in question in a probation box and come back to it later.

Too much/too little time: When I work with people who are working or volunteering part time, with mothers working at raising children, and with home-based office workers, I sometimes find we have to put a little more structure in their days. They enjoyed the freedom and flexibility at first, but too much flexibility can be difficult to manage. I went through this when I started my own business. So we add some structure (and time) for home or office organization into the days. They are happier. They get more done. And the tasks that are part of everyday living are less of a big deal to get done; more time is spent on family time, fun, the passion of the work, etc. So consider how much structure you have to your days. Maybe you need a little more. Go back to page 59 for ideas on how to work organizing into a varied schedule.

FINDING MOTIVATION

You've decided where to start and when you will organize. Now how do you follow through and finish the journey? Here are some ideas to help you stay motivated and accomplish your goals.

Organizing requires a lot of mental and physical energy. These ideas will help to keep you motivated during those times when you feel too tired, too overwhelmed, or too frustrated to continue.

Find a Great Place for Your Donations

It's far easier to let go of your belongings and items you once cherished when you know the item will be going to a worthy new home. You can take comfort knowing that the object will enrich someone else's life as much as it did yours. See chapter six for specific ideas on how to find places to donate.

When you donate, you are involving others in your organizing process—the first *I* in SIMPLIFY. Donating to a group close to your heart will also help you let go without regrets—the *L* in SIMPLIFY. You will have no regrets about giving something away when you know it is furthering a cause you believe in.

Find Your Inspiration

You no doubt have a goal for reorganizing. Use this goal as your motivation. Make your goal tangible in the form of a picture, an inspirational quote, a before picture, or a vision board. One man I worked with was chief babysitter for his grandson. He wanted to reorganize his home office/radio hobby space into a space for his grandson to learn about the radio hobby, so on his desk he kept a photo of himself with his grandson to remind himself of why he was working on the room.

Other ways to stay inspired:

- Tell your friends.
- Spend time volunteering wherever you are donating items.
- Journal. Use this statement as a writing prompt: When my room is more organized and simplified, I will be able to …
- Tell your support groups or community of colleagues.
- Reread a chapter of this book
- Take an organizing or downsizing class while you're working on your space.
- Hire a Certified Organizer Coach® or Certified Professional Organizer® to work with you once a month. They will inspire you to keep working and praise you for all you've done.

"There are basically two types of people … 'The throwers' relish the experience of clearing out and moving on … and 'the keepers' … compelled to preserve special things and memories … One will downsize quickly … The other will linger over the process … balance these attributes, and call on them when appropriate."

– LINDA HETZER AND JANET HULSTRAND, *MOVING ON*

Work With Someone

Unless you are a very private person, you may find it helpful to occasionally invite someone to work with you in certain rooms or when sorting particular belongings. This is the first *I* in SIMPLIFY—involve others.

For example, when dealing with sentimental belongings, it might be easier for you to make decisions if you have someone to tell the stories to.

If your partner has the opposite disposition when it comes to organizing, it can be hard for you to understand his or her point of view. Both skills are needed during your process if you are downsizing, for example. Be aware of your differences if you choose to reorganize with your partner.

Telling stories revives the memories and allows you to let go of the object.

If you know someone who could possibly use the items you are purging, consider inviting them over to select things they would like before you donate the items. One couple I worked with was downsizing for a move. Their son was about to get married, so they asked their future daughter-in-law to work with them in the kitchen with the idea that she could select items for her new kitchen from the items they were parting with. Imagine how good the couple felt knowing that the things they were getting rid of would go to such a welcoming new home (not to mention how much they enjoyed the bonding time with a new family member).

Women will often invite over another woman friend or friends when it's time to go through clothing. Choose someone who will be honest about what really does or doesn't look good on you. If you want to pass your clothes on to your friend, choose someone who is your same size and has admired your taste in clothes.

Choose an organizing buddy who will not judge but will gently assist you in making your decisions. You're reorganizing for you, not for someone else. And working with someone who is even slightly judgmental will cause decisions you'll regret later. You need to take your time.

Organizing is like finances with couples. One of you may be a saver, and one spends more freely. One of you finds it easy to get rid of things; the other holds on to things for sentimental or practical reasons. If your partner has the opposite disposition when it comes to organizing, it can be hard for you to understand his or her point of view. Both skills are needed during your process if you are downsizing, for example. Be aware of your differences if you choose to reorganize with your partner.

Manufacture Deadlines

To get yourself started and to keep yourself going on this reorganizing journey, it's helpful to build in some deadlines. If you set deadlines around important dates, it is a bit harder to break those deadlines than it is to break the ones you arbitrarily set on the calendar.

Examples of manufactured deadlines include:

Holidays: You could decide to go through all your jewelry before a certain holiday because you want to pass along your old favorite pieces of jewelry to the women in your family.

Family reunions: You can make it your goal to go through all your photos before a family reunion. Then you'll either have a box of photos to give to each relative, or you'll have made an album or scrapbook that you can show to family members.

Visitors: Welcoming guests into your home is a great motivation for organizing. It's part of the *I* in SIMPLY—involving others. One woman reorganized her guest room in time for visitors who were coming at Thanksgiving. The room had been where she put everything she didn't have a permanent home for.

Another woman decided to invite her friends over to celebrate her birthday. She called them ahead of time so it was a firm commitment and she would be accountable for completing the job before her birthday.

Another woman reorganized her kitchen as well as her household central (papers/bills system) in time for her quarterly lunch with her female friends.

Appointments: One woman made a weekly appointment at her consignment shop until she finished weeding out all the clothes. Being accountable to others can be a very strong source of motivation.

Take a look at your calendar for the next few months. What manufactured deadlines can you come up with?

Rewards, Big and Small

It's tempting to dream of a big reward or gift you'll give yourself after you've finished reorganizing your entire home. I suggest you think small this time. Your first reward can be an emotional one and one you give yourself: the gift of time—time to focus on yourself and your move into your next life chapter. People often find, too, that the reward of a clear space is reward enough and keeps them motivated to move on to the next step. It's important to break down an overwhelmingly large project into small steps. Reward yourself for completing each step. You know yourself best, and so you'll know just how many rewards you'll need along the way to spur you on. Reorganizing is a lot more enjoyable if you have glimmers of fun and hope along the way to enjoy the journey!

Think about a new reward as you complete each project. Research shows humans are far more motivated by smaller, more frequent rewards rather than waiting for one bigger reward at the end of the major project. So if the major project is reorganizing your home and your life, reward yourself each time you complete a smaller related project.

> Research shows humans are far more motivated by smaller, more frequent rewards rather than waiting for one bigger reward at the end of the major project.

Ideas for rewards. Here are some rewards my clients have given themselves:

- Time to work on their organizing projects—which results in the most wonderful feelings, once a cleared space is done. The payoff is the freeing feeling you have when you see the completed space and get to enjoy your vision for the room.
- Dinner out at a nicer-than-usual restaurant

- Wine with friends
- A new book
- Inviting friends over to enjoy the new space created by reorganizing
- New speakers for music
- A print to hang on the wall of the new studio or craft space
- A museum trip
- A concert
- A walk outside

Certainly, you will feel rewarded as you donate your previously favorite belongings to give them new homes. What can you do for yourself, though, to enjoy the feeling of accomplishment before you move on to your next reorganizing project?

Hire a Certified Professional Organizer® or a Certified Organizer Coach®

Professional organizers are accountability partners who can keep you going when reorganizing gets difficult or when life seems to get in the way. We know how to get you started, keep you motivated, and assist you to the finish line when you are not sure you can make it. We work on the systems to prevent the clutter from returning. We work on moving obstacles out of your path. We work on motivation. See the Resources page at the back of the book for more information on working with a Certified Professional Organizer®.

Now that you have your motivation and a structured plan for when you will organize, you can begin the actual work of reorganizing. The first step is to take a tour of your home to evaluate it and set objectives (the first *E* and *O* of REORGANIZE). I'll walk you through this process in the next chapter.

PART TWO

Reorganize Your Surroundings

THIS SECTION COVERS THE SIMPLIFYING AND REORGANIZING PROCESS, which begins with taking a tour of your home. Using the Home Is Not a Home Without chart, you'll visit each room with a new set of eyes. You'll answer questions that help you identify the function of each room and find ways to completely change the function of a room, such as transforming a dining room into a home office. Now is your opportunity to start fresh.

You'll also find support in making the tough decisions of what to let go of and what to keep. With no-regrets decisions, you'll feel good about the new homes you create for your belongings, whether they are staying in your house or going to someone else.

5. Evaluate Your Home and Establish Your Objectives

AS YOU PREPARE TO PHYSICALLY REORGANIZE your house and your belongings, I want you to take a tour of your home. This is a surface-level tour and should only take about an hour, so don't go into all the nooks and crannies yet. You're going to survey each room. It's not the time to evaluate the contents of every drawer or cupboard in the room. You need to know where you are heading, and identify the best spots to stop along the way, before you can set out on your journey. This is the first step I always take with a client, provided he or she is comfortable showing me the entire house.

Bring the following items with you on your tour:

☐ Your answers to the Create a Vision for Your Organizing Efforts exercise in chapter two (page 35). They can be written down, remembered in your head, or on an audio recording.

☐ The Room Tour Questions in the appendix (page 206).

☐ The Home is Not Home Without Chart in the appendix (page 208).

☐ A notebook or handheld audio recorder to complete the chart and capture any thoughts, decisions, or ideas that come to you as you tour.

SURVEY THE ROOM AS A WHOLE

The goal of this tour is to quickly evaluate your home and decide what organizing projects need to be done. You can do the tour all at once or tour one room a day if your time is limited. This is the first *E* and the *O* in the REORGANIZE acronym from chapter two (evaluate and objectives). Start your evaluation by asking yourself the same basic set of questions in each room or space. These room tour questions can also be found on page 208 in the appendix.

1. What do you see?
2. What do people comment on when they arrive?
3. What kind of energy do you feel in this spot?
4. What's in place?
5. What is out of place?
6. What activities go on here right now?
7. What activities no longer occur here even though the stuff associated with those activities is still located here?
8. What activities would you like to have happen here but don't today because of clutter or space or other considerations?
9. What frustrates you about this area?
10. Do you enjoy the color scheme?
11. What systems are important to have here, and are they working for you today? (Sometimes it is helpful to answer this with a 1–10 scale, 10 being perfect. Usually, some parts of the system *are* working; it's not the whole system that's failed you.)
12. How would you like this space to be?

Each room has had a purpose in the past, but each room can have a new purpose now, based on what's important to you in this chapter of your life. This reorganization is about having your home reflect who you are now and who you are becoming. We need to make physical space for current and new interests. Give yourself the freedom to let go of your old interests and embrace your new ones.

EVALUATE THE CONTENTS OF EACH ROOM

After you answer the room tour questions and have made some decisions about the future functions of the area, you can begin to evaluate the contents of the room using the Home is Not Home Without Chart. Identify the objects in the room that positively align with your answers to the room tour questions and list them on your Home Is Not Home Without Chart.

The chart and the questions that accompany it are designed to help you think differently about your belongings and your space. You are changing. You'll want your space and organizing systems to reflect this change and be in sync with who you are becoming. Use the questions to help you decide which items from the past are still part of who you are today and which items are not anymore. In another chapter of your life, you may have had a passion for quilting or for history books. They were wonderful for that chapter, but if they are not current interests, can you let them go?

On the chart, list the items that are still important to you and that you know you want to keep in your life. You can think of these as your favorite things.

Some people will want to complete the Home is Not Home Without Chart as they walk through their home with it. Others prefer to walk around their houses and then sit down with the chart later. Either approach works; it just depends on your thinking and processing style. Or you might take two tours, filling out the chart on your second time through the house. Stand in each room and acknowledge what makes the room feel like home to you. This will be your first cut at identifying the items that need to stay in your home as you're reorganizing for your next chapter.

Identify Your Least Favorite Items

Quite recently, a woman in one of my downsizing classes told me it would be easier for her to select her nonfavorites, those items she was certain

Home is Not Home Without ...

EXAMPLE ROOM	EXAMPLE DESCRIPTION
Hallway or Entryway	The table we put our things on when we come in the house. The bowl on top that was Grandma's.
Bedroom 2	The matching nightstands I bought for our daughter so many years ago. A few of the family photos she framed.
Bedroom 3	Antique beds. The tole-painted washstand.
Bedroom 4 or Office	Files from my career. Selected books. My desk chair and my desk. Fabrics for quilt projects. Fabrics bought on our travels.
Master Bedroom	My favorite quilt I made while the kids were growing up.
Kitchen	Favorite pots, pans, and recipes I use most often. Family recipes. The statue from our trip to Europe.
Laundry Area	Organizing bins I use for all the laundry stuff.
Dining Room	Silverware. Some of the china plates passed down. Favorite wine glasses collected from our travels.
Home Office	The desk I love from my favorite store that works well with my style and habits. The pictures on the wall for inspiration. My favorite, most comfortable desk chair, old as it is.
Bathroom	The framed picture of all of us on a beach vacation. The baskets I found during that neat trip we took to a Shaker village.
Living Room	Paintings. The loveseat that's so much more comfortable than the couch! The needlepoint coasters from my great-aunt.
Den	Certain books I love to reread. My favorite reading chair.
Attic	Selected books and artwork of the kids. Mom's jewelry box.
Basement	Exercise equipment. Selected tools.
Garage/Shed	Tools from Dad. My gardening things.

she could remove from her house, instead of immediately picking her very favorite items. I'd never considered that approach before, but it certainly has its merits, and as I said, what matters most is that the system works for you. So try completing the Home is Not Home Without Chart, and if you're really stuck and cannot choose items that make home feel like home, then identify the things you know you don't want and see how you feel about the remaining items. We all think differently, so there's no one-size-fits-all way to do this. One of the benefits to working with a Certified Professional Organizer® or Certified Organizer Coach® is that we'll collaborate with you to match your thinking and processing styles with the many possibilities available to organize your life.

TOURING ROOM BY ROOM

After you gather up all the items you need for the tour, you can start working your way through the house. In addition to a general room tour of questions, some rooms will have unique questions you'll ask yourself. I've included these questions, listed room by room.

Entryway

This is not the formal entrance, but wherever you enter the house each day. It is often the same place where close friends are welcomed into your home. First go out the entry door and then come back into your home. What does your entryway say to you when you walk in the house? What kind of first impression does this entryway give? Answer the room tour questions based on how you feel when you immediately enter the house. This is a frequent starting point because the first look sets your mood as you walk into your home.

Spare Bedrooms

Do you have bedrooms set up for your grown children to return home? When was the last time one of them stayed over? Is there a possibility of

Don't Toss it All

Your initial home tour is *not* a time to say to yourself that you "just want to move on and start fresh." Please do not make this an intellectual exercise by ignoring feelings and tossing out too many things simply because you're in reorganizing mode.

The house did not become cluttered or stop serving your needs overnight, and it's not going to take one reorganizing session to bring things back to the way they used to be. Remember what I said about reorganizing: It's cathartic and therapeutic. So it's not just about moving things around and giving things away; it's about *giving you* the time you likely need to deal with the internal work.

It's a pretty exciting journey if you're really on board. So enjoy it and don't rush it. It's the journey, not the destination; the destination may change as you make the journey if you let it.

If you need to go through your life partner's things because he or she has died, you particularly need to take your time. This is a time to grieve if you need to. Be patient with yourself. Be patient with others who may wish to help but don't know the best way to help. They are well meaning.

Sometimes you'll need to revisit a room or a collection at a later date. Getting rid of someone's belongings does not get rid of your anger or sadness; only processing your feelings will do that. So please tread carefully here. The Home is Not Home Without Chart can assist you in those very clear decisions, to keep or not to keep. The gray decisions, the "I'm-not-totally-sure" types of decisions, come later with more time and further assistance from this book. If your emotions about specific items are too strong for you to think clearly, leave the items where they are or carefully pack them away and put them in storage until you can address them properly.

having them share the room with one of your newest hobbies or your home office? Organize your rooms for their most frequent uses.

I once worked with a woman who made beautiful jewelry. Her craft space had been in the basement from the time her children were born. It was a nice getaway space when needed. But now, the space was always a little cold, a little damp, and the lighting was not strong enough for detailed craft work.

A room without a purpose can become a catch-all space. It's the "I-don't-know-what-to-do-with-this-thing-so-I'll-put-it-in-here-for-now" room.

Her life transition was as a new empty nester. She was in the reinvention phase of her life, working on creating her next chapter. When we worked together, I listened and took in her comments about the basement as her jewelry space. It had served her well for many years. She wanted a studio with better natural light, improved storage for the beads and her tools, and a design space separate from her working space. She'd done her crafting in the basement for so long that it was difficult for her to think about her upstairs space in a different way. I gradually introduced the idea of using her grown child's bedroom as her studio, while keeping a bed in there for overnight guests.

So for grown children's bedrooms, think about how often the room is used as a bedroom. How often does it stay empty and unused? The house is 100 percent yours now, so do whatever you'd like. You'll find new ways to accommodate family visits, the grandchild who stays over, or the guest from afar. Think about activities that take place somewhere else in the house. Could you make space in a bedroom for that activity? Some options include a home office, household office and bill-paying center, off-season storage, or a student setup for yourself if you're going back to school.

There's another reason to set a new purpose for each of your unused or now vacant rooms (and this applies to closets, too): A room without a purpose can become a catchall space. It's the "I-don't-know-what-to-do-with-this-thing-so-I'll-put-it-in-here-for-now" room. This room's name always gets a laugh, and I'm guessing it's a laugh of recognition.

On the flip side, have you been using your spare bedroom as a craft room or home office, but now you are welcoming a new, permanent resident into your home—be it a new baby, an aging parent, a grown child, or other adult relative who needs to stay with you for a while? If this is the case, you'll need to relinquish this area to give them privacy. You'll need to find another room to house these activities.

Master Bedroom

The master bedroom can be especially difficult if you're widowed or divorced. This is the most intimate of spaces and would have been the main space the two of you shared, but now you are alone. Regardless of the reasons you are alone, whether they were forced on you or you chose to be on your own, this is an emotionally difficult room.

Questions unique to the master bedroom are:

- How much of your past is represented in the colors, the fabrics, and the furniture?
- If I walked into your space, how many mementos and memories would I see out in the open, atop the armoire and bureaus, on the bookshelves, or on the walls?
- Are you still comfortable with these memories, or have some outlived their meaning to you? Which are your favorites you'll always want around you? Which are questionable? Which no longer mean what they once did—or make you realize you're ready to move on?
- How long has it been since your partner was here? Have you taken out only a few of his or her belongings or several? Or are you just beginning?
- What have you always wanted in your bedroom, but compromised so you don't have it? One of my clients preferred to keep laundry baskets in her bedroom, but had compromised with her partner

to keep them in the hallway. Another client had always wanted a nightstand to hold the books she read in bed, but her husband had never wanted them because they attracted clutter.

I've often heard from clients that their well-meaning mother, father, siblings, or friend told them to just get rid of it all because it will make you feel better. That's not necessarily true. There is a much easier way to process your grief and still move on: Go through memories in stages. Ignore what "they" tell you and listen to your heart and what makes you comfortable. Do what's right for you to be sure you're making no-regrets decisions.

Main closet and bureaus. While in your master bedroom, look through closets, the bureau, and any other area that will need an intensive organizing effort. As you look through your things, ask:

- How do you feel about your wardrobe? What percentage of your total clothing collection do you wear on a regular basis?
- Does all of your clothing fit? If you plan to lose weight to get back into a smaller size, will the smaller clothing still be in fashion when you reach that goal, or would it be better to reward yourself with a new wardrobe?
- What does your ideal closet look like?
- How can you create more room in your closet?

If you are dealing with the loss of your partner, look through their closets and anywhere they kept clothing. Ask yourself:

1. How ready am I to move things out of this room? Can I move things out in stages? One woman was ready to give away her husband's clothes to favorite friends and family members about six months after he died. Her husband had been a sharp dresser. It delighted her when she'd occasionally see a friend or family member wearing one of his tweed blazers, heavy winter shirts, or a suit. She didn't need the clothing to remind her of this aspect of her husband, so this stage came quickly for her.

   After that, things slowed down. She waited about another

two years before she went through other possessions: memorabilia from his youth, baseball memories he'd kept over the years, books, and more.

2. What was the *essence* of this person (passions, hobbies, philosophies of life, favorite paintings or prints or books)? Who was this person? If you can answer this question, you can select a group of favorite items from their belongings to hold on to. This is an excellent case of keeping a few key items so that less becomes more. Fewer objects still give you the memories, but give you more mental and physical space for your next chapter.

Kitchen

Home is not home without ... In a kitchen, this can take on different meanings, depending on your situation and how you once spent your time here. One man, divorced and with joint custody of his children, had always wanted to be the cook in the family. He loved experimenting and sharing his cooking at dinner parties. But during his marriage, he had few opportunities to cook.

Because so many activities happen in the kitchen, it can also become a dumping ground for paperwork, items coming into the home, and items that need to leave your home.

After the divorce, and after he'd figured out a bit about being a single parent, he took a tour of his kitchen. He wanted the kitchen to become a central gathering spot for the family instead of seeing his children disappear into their rooms after school. His favorite items all had to do with being a chef, entertaining family and friends more often, and making the kitchen and family room space friendlier for his kids to play in, with or without him around.

Because so many activities happen in the kitchen, it can also become a dumping ground for paperwork, items coming into the home, and items that need to leave your home. As you tour the room ask:

- What activities occur here that could be moved to a different room? This could include sorting the mail, paying bills, and organizing items to take out of the home (library books, merchandise to return, items that need to be repaired, etc.).

Laundry Area

The main life transition questions for the laundry area or room center around whether the number of household members has changed. If you've added a parent, child, grandchild, or are a host family, does your current space function well? Is your folding space large enough, and do you have enough shelving to handle your laundry products? Does everyone in the house understand the expectations for this area? What can you do to make it easier for people to sort dirty laundry and then put away clean clothes?

Sometimes people store their household cleaning products in the laundry room or use shelves for household storage. Do you have enough room for these items? Are dangerous items properly stored so children and pets can't get to them?

Dining Room

Dining rooms vary widely from home to home. In homes with small kitchens, the dining room is the main (or only) place to eat at a table, so it is used frequently. If this is the case in your home, treat this room as an extension of the kitchen. A key question is:

- How can I keep the table free from clutter so it is always available for dining?

In homes with eat-in kitchens, the dining room may be more formal and used only on special occasions. If this is the case in your home, answer these questions to help you identify your favorite belongings:

- How often do you want to entertain? Is someone else hosting family holiday dinners now?

- When you entertain, are you entertaining in this room because you enjoy it or because you want to use the space?
- What's the typical size of the groups you entertain?

Many people repurpose their dining rooms. This area can be used as a home office, a study, a craft room, or homework space for yourself or your grandchildren. As we grow older, people tend to entertain in smaller groups, entertain less formally, or dine out instead of hosting a dinner party. If your dining room is largely unused, think of ways you can transform it into a space that you will use at least once a week. Look at your goals and dreams for this next chapter of your life and decide how this space can help you achieve them. One woman uses her dining room as a library and household office.

If your dining room is largely unused, think of ways you can transform it into a space that you will use at least once a week. Look at your goals and dreams for this next chapter of your life and decide how this space can help you achieve them.

As an aside, if you repurpose your dining room (which is a wonderful idea if it helps you use the space), change it back to its traditional purpose before you put your house up for sale because proper staging helps houses sell faster. But don't let this future consideration keep you from enjoying your space today.

Formal dining rooms also often contain items such as your most delicate or expensive belongings and items inherited from one or more relatives—china, furniture, collectibles. Sometimes, inherited items become favorites, but other times they were gifts that you graciously accepted but never really wanted. Perhaps you had the feeling that the relative was just trying to declutter her stuff by giving it to you. Now is the time to think about what's really a favorite and use those favorites or put them on display.

There are three key ways to enjoy an object: use it, display it, or give it away knowing it will have a new, loving home. If we can't enjoy an object, why do we let it take up physical and mental space?

If you suspect an item is valuable, have it appraised before you decide to keep it, donate it, or sell it so you can make the best decision. If you decide to keep something because it is valuable, be sure you are able to care for it or store it in a way that protects its value, and have the item insured.

Home Office

Which activities do *you* want to work on in your home office space?

Or, ask the question the opposite way: Where would you like to do your work and take care of your household management responsibilities? Here are some questions to ask as you evaluate your home office:

> If you decide to keep something because it is valuable, be sure you are able to care for it or store it in a way that protects its value, and have the item insured.

- How do I prefer to work? Do you like to spread out and therefore need a lot of room? Do you like to have separate areas for different responsibilities? You can create separate spaces within the same room. One client who ran a small business decided she needed to separate the bill-paying activities from her more creative and management-centered business activities. She set up a separate desk to use when she handles bills and some other administrative activities. For her, as with many people, physically separating the space helps to set her mind in the appropriate mode, whether it's creative, management, or bill paying.
- Can I work without distractions? Can you work without interruption in this area? Is it quiet enough for you to concentrate in? Or, if you are social, is it in an area where you won't feel isolated?
- How does the décor affect the energy in the room? Colors affect

our inspiration, motivation, and mood, as does lighting. You may want to make repainting the room and changing the lighting a long-term goal for this area.

- How can I get other household members to respect this area? Make your office space separate from the rest of the house, or you'll spend time cleaning up, readjusting, and finding things every time someone else uses the space. That's not really motivating to get to the work you really want to do and are passionate about, is it? A new office space deserves a discussion with family about office hours, computer time, interruptions, personal calls, and so forth.

Paperwork Around the House

While we're talking about the home office, let's assess your paperwork situation, whether currently all in one room or scattered around the house. What is it about papers that makes them so dreaded? They are often the most difficult things to organize. I have two theories as to why this is the case. Can you relate to either or both?

First, many papers represent something going on in your life—an invitation to an event you might attend, a certificate you've earned, a thank-you card for something generous you did, and so forth. They are a mosaic of your life and give you some part of the picture of your life. So let's figure out how to deal with them and give them the respect they need as part of your life.

Second, we think of and talk about papers as if they're all alike, even though they are vastly different and require different responses. Bills need to be paid and then filed for future reference if they're tax related. Some paperwork requires decisions—advertisements, invitations, and so on. Letting them sit around is a way of delaying a decision—will you buy the product, will you attend the event? Some are sentimental, like cards. Different types of paperwork require different methods of organizing.

Answer these six questions about your papers, and you'll begin to craft your method to organize them.

1. What kinds of papers do you save?
2. For *each* group of papers you're saving, what do you plan to *do* with the group? Why do you save them?
3. How often will you need to use what you've saved for each group?
4. Are you a paper person, or are you moving more toward saving info on your computer? It helps to move one way or the other so you don't have to check both paper and electronic files.
5. Where will you gather and use the information?
6. How often will you need to access the file? This will determine *where* you put the file.

Find more about this in chapter ten.

Bathrooms

Bathrooms would seem to be easy to reorganize, but this space can be challenging as we age. As you evaluate your bathrooms, consider the following:

- How many people currently live in your home? The number of people living in your home changes over time. If you are in the so-called empty-nest phase, with fewer people, there's less of a need for so many bath products, sheets, and towels. So knowing the number of people can help you set a boundary for yourself, for example, to have just two sets of sheets for each bed, or three sets of bath towels (more if you have houseguests often).
- What, if any, are the current physical or medical challenges faced by those who use the bathroom? For young children, it's potty training, not being able to reach the sink, and the need to child-proof the room. For the elderly, it's mobility issues and risk of falls. If someone in your home has mobility issues, identify how high

and low they can comfortably reach, and organize so all of their items are within this range. You may need to purge items so everything will fit in this space. If you've developed a new medical or health challenge, ask yourself how much space you'll need for medicines and other paraphernalia. Because of the high humidity and temperature changes, the bathroom isn't always the best place to keep medication. More helpful would be storing these items nearer to where they are used, particularly if there are mobility issues. Medicines might be appropriate in the kitchen, if taken at mealtimes, for example.

- How long do you expect to stay in this home? Consider incremental improvements to your bathroom before you consider any major renovation. For example, if you are taking care of someone older or someone who is in and out of the hospital fairly frequently, what are his or her daily needs? Can you reorganize so the individual needs only to live on one floor?

An elderly couple lived on their own in the family home, where they felt many years of history and great sentimental attachment. They felt strongly about staying in their home, and their belief was "family takes care of family." When the wife's health issues worsened and her mobility lessened, her husband and children started thinking about a renovation to allow her to live only on the first floor. The house was fairly old, so the layout was not very flexible. This change would require quite a major renovation, which would cause too much stress and disruption. The family decided to reorganize instead of renovate and asked me to help.

Once we broke down the wife's daily routine and realized how little she really needed, we were able to create new organizing systems that supported her on the first floor by adding railings in several rooms to assist her mobility, moving linens downstairs, and decluttering space under the first-floor bathroom sink for them. We also brought down some of her clothing, and her husband got into a routine of helping his wife get dressed daily, so he brought down her choice of clothes. She could not get into the tub, so she figured out a washing routine using the downstairs bath. All of this was a reorganization to support what mattered most to the family, caring for loved ones at home.

Living Spaces: Living Room or Den

This is an area of the house where we spend a lot of our time, no matter what our family structure is. This is a space you'll want to spend time on to not only reorganize, but also to redecorate. Imagine a new furniture style or new colors as your life changes. Parents of a new baby and young children need durable, stain-resistant furniture and carpet. Empty nesters may want to add more elegance or change their color scheme now that their home will experience less wear and tear.

Karen bought her beautiful 150-year-old house with her husband, and they'd spent many hours making it their own. They ended up divorcing before this space was finished and decorated. Karen called because she was ready to move on, by herself, and she needed to make the house her own. She realized on our tour that her only favorite items in the living room were the natural light, the wooden floors, selected knitting books, and all of her yarn. The rest of the objects had more meaning to her ex-husband, and she'd never had any real attachment to them.

We use the basement and attic to store things for which we can't make decisions. Make it your goal to make as many decisions about these items as possible.

Basement and Attic

If items have been relegated to the "black hole" of the house (which is what so many people consider the basement), then how is it you're enjoying them? We often store things in these spaces because we want to save them for use someday. With all that you've gone through, is "someday" today? Consider the financial and sentimental value of things you've put in these two spaces. We also use these spaces to store things for which we can't make decisions. Make it your goal to make as many decisions about these items as possible. You really have two choices, keep the item and put it to use or on display *or* get rid of the item.

Holiday and seasonal decorations do belong in this space, but even with these, think about which are your favorites. Identify any objects you keep because of guilt or obligation. What is the worst that will happen if you get rid of them? Also consider how much decorating you plan to do in the future. If you will be celebrating the holidays elsewhere, you may find you need or want to do very little decorating. Give yourself permission to let go of things you no longer need or use.

The attic and basement both tend to be storage for your childhood memorabilia and your children's childhood memorabilia. Jot down on your chart how many boxes of childhood items you think you have. Don't go through them yet. Just estimate how much you have so you know what to expect.

Speaking from personal experience, grown children do forget what Mom and Dad are saving or storing for them. They know they can always go home for their stuff, but to go through it and make decisions is too hard or too time-consuming. Children believe their parents have extra space now that all the kids are gone, so they just leave their stuff there until their parents say something.

Parents often save much more than their children end up wanting. Generations are different in regard to the things they acquire and how they acquire them, their tolerance for used versus new, how much they can afford on their own, and the state of the items (think prints of photographs versus digital photos). Much changes, so it's better to ask what the children want to keep rather than assume, and it gives you permission to let go if they say no.

Garage and Shed

As you look through the garage and shed ask these specific questions:

- Do you need room to work on your car?
- Do you still participate in all the sports that you have equipment for?
- How much outdoor work will you do on your own?

If your life situation has changed, the answers to all three questions probably recently changed, too. Or maybe you'll decide you want to try doing some things for yourself now if you suddenly have more time in your schedule. Go for it. Give yourself a season or two and see how it makes you feel. You may love the idea of taking care of your own home and having control over the maintenance schedule. I gave this a try in my own life and ended up loving it!

WHERE TO START

Now that you've toured your home and answered specific questions about each room, you may have already discovered where you want to start reorganizing.

For other people, the tour will have helped you identify your favorite items, but your question still remains: Which space do I start with? Allow me to give you some suggestions and, of course, questions to ask yourself to help you figure this out.

Please start simply. The momentum you carry from earlier successes will give you encouragement to work through the difficult tasks.

Start Easy

You can choose whichever room or collection or space seems the easiest. This will give you a quick success that you can brag about (even if it's only to yourself).

This is very motivating and makes you feel good. It shows you that you *can* do this. And that's a great feeling to have as you start on a second project.

Don't Start With the Most Difficult Areas

You might think you'll start with a difficult project thinking, *if I can do this, I can do anything.* But starting here can be a recipe for discouragement and feelings of failure. This is a time to build on smaller successes. You may also still be dealing with the emotions or logistics of the life transition you are experiencing. Organizing is about making decisions on everything, and that can be draining. You may lose motivation because it may be too hard to do on your own. It may be too complicated; there may be too many different types of belongings, making it too hard to find new homes for everything.

Please start simply. The momentum you carry from earlier successes will give you encouragement to work through the difficult tasks. Plus if you save the most difficult until the end, you can take all the time you need, knowing that the rest of your house is already reorganized.

Listen to Your Inner Voice

What do you think about your home? What do you know you love? What do you know about what you want going forward? What do you wish for? Sometimes this will tell you which space bothers you the most or which space is the one in which to create something new. Worried where you'll put things you take out of one room? Maybe you need to start by clearing out wherever their new homes will be (their receiving area).

Theresa wanted to start in her bedroom, which was located on the second floor of her home. She was a new mother and had recently moved into a new home. These transitions had caused her bedroom to become the place where all the clutter from the downstairs was deposited during rushed cleanups. Master bedrooms commonly become dumping grounds because they are large rooms that are off-limits to guests. We genuinely intend to clear the space after the guests are gone, but we are busy, and when the room doesn't get cleared out once or twice, the piles seem insurmountable.

Theresa wanted to reclaim the bedroom as an adult space instead of a storage area. She also knew a fair amount of the clothing cluttering her closet would be maternity clothes, and she and her husband didn't plan to have more children. So this would be an easy place to start, and even easier after we decided on a family-oriented organization she could donate items to.

She wanted to go upstairs at night and be calmer. She believed the chaos in her bedroom affected her sleeping and her health. Starting in her room would bring her the most satisfaction and immediately improve her attitude about her home, so this is where she decided to start.

> You're reorganizing your house for you first. Work on where you want to start. You're the one who needs to keep at it, so choose somewhere that means something to you.

Listen to What Your Family Says

Do you hear, "I'm so frustrated." "I can't work in here!" "I can never find … " "We bought another one?!" and so forth from your family? You can start with the areas that cause your family members frustration. A quick caution if this sounds attractive: You're reorganizing your house for you first. Work on where you want to start. You're the one who needs to keep at it, so choose somewhere that means something to you. How much more motivating is it to work on turning an extra room into your craft space versus working on the kitchen cabinets because your daughter says you *should* have more organized cabinets?

Take a Seasonal Approach

If you really can't decide where to start, slot in rooms that have climate issues first—attic, basement, garage, and shed—so you're not working on the attic in 90-degree weather for example. Then think about your manufactured deadlines. Which ones help you decide on a month for other rooms? Do you need to clear guest rooms for summer visitors? Are you hosting a holiday event and need to clear the dining room and kitchen?

SELECT THE SIZE OR SCALE OF YOUR PROJECT

Before you jump in, remember you can organize in stages and break things down into smaller steps. This is the *M* in the SIMPLIFY acronym from chapter two—make small steps. There are essentially three options for the scale of your project: a room, a collection, or a receiving area.

A collection isn't limited to collectibles or objects that are designated as a collection. In this context, it means an entire category of like items. Your entire wardrobe constitutes a collection, as does your paperwork, your dishware, your craft items, your books, your movies, the food in your pantry or freezer, and so on. These objects may currently all be in one room, but I more often find that the collection has spread throughout the house, which causes stress for the collection's owner and other household members.

A receiving area is the place where things you don't need in your everyday spaces will be stored for occasional use or future use. It could be a dresser, a set of shelves, a pantry, or a closet. Some people use a barn, off-site storage, or even on-site storage. My client Serena felt more comfortable clearing and organizing the receiving area first because she felt it would be easier going through the everyday spaces in the house knowing she'd already made room to receive items from them.

We've covered a lot in this chapter. After you finish your house tour and complete your Home is Not Home Without Chart, you should know exactly where you are going to start and have scheduled time to start reorganizing. In the next chapter we head to the actual space you want to work on. We'll go through the next few steps of the REORGANIZE process together.

6. Deciding What to Keep and What to Remove

IT'S TIME TO BEGIN THE PHYSICAL ACT OF ORGANIZING, but don't think that the preparation you did in the earlier chapters doesn't count. The work you've done up to this point has equipped you with a realistic plan for success. The careful thought you've devoted to this project will help you work more efficiently and make the decision-making process easier. This chapter deals with the second *R* and *G* of REORGANIZE—"round and round" and "get rid of (or not)." You'll be removing objects from the area you are working in and making decisions about whether or not to keep each item in the space. It sounds like a big task—but you have prepared yourself for it. At the end of your organizing session, you will feel energized by the progress you are making.

Before you get started, take a photo of the area you are about to work on so you can mark the progress you've made. There is something about photographs; they tell a truer story than our memories or our subjective eyes allow us to see.

Before we start, a quick word about perfectionism, and I know it well because I've been there. Learn to outsmart yourself. If you're having trouble making decisions, think about temporary, transitional solutions. Or think about my favorite phrase, "one step closer." You may not be able to make a final decision, but if you can make part of the decision or create a probation area, then you've moved yourself one step closer to where you want to be.

SETTING UP

As you begin organizing, these are the materials and supplies you'll want on hand:

- [ ] Camera: for before and after pictures
- [ ] Your inspiration: a picture of your future dream space or who you're doing this for, a written explanation of why you are doing this, or an inspirational quote
- [ ] Your completed Room Tour Questions for the area
- [ ] Your completed Home is Not Home Without Chart
- [ ] Notebook/plans
- [ ] Music or an audio book
- [ ] Timer, if you intend to work for a specific amount of time
- [ ] Snacks, water
- [ ] Boxes or plastic bins: Use plastic bins if you plan to store belongings. Use boxes for items leaving your house.
- [ ] Tags, stickers, labels: It's easy to forget from one day to the next which box was for recycling and which was for donating. Always mark your boxes/bins/bags, or you'll be shaking your head when you have to relook at the items to figure out the purposes of each box.
- [ ] Markers
- [ ] Trash bags
- [ ] Scissors
- [ ] This book

I also suggest you bring a phone with you. If possible, avoid answering the phone while you work, but keep it nearby if you have someone who relies on you in an emergency.

Identify Your Receiving Areas

Before you start, identify where your holding areas will be. You will need a holding area for the boxes of items that are leaving your home, whether you are donating them, giving them to friends and family, or disposing of them. Some people will take the boxes directly to their cars, which makes it harder to revisit the box's contents and moves them one step closer to delivering the box to its final destination. If you forget about things in your trunk, write yourself a note on an errands pad or a sticky note, and keep it near your dashboard in plain view. Schedule a time on your calendar to make the trip.

Other people hire an errand service to take away boxes to donation or consignment. Having someone else finish the work of removing the items can be a relief after making so many organizing decisions.

You'll also need a holding area in each room of your home. I suggest you simply place a box labeled "Keep in (name of room)" in each room. You will fill this box with items that you have moved from other rooms in your home as you organize those rooms. You can find a specific home in the room for each item when you are ready to organize that room. This keeps you focused on one task at a time and takes the pressure off of you to find homes for everything at once, which can be overwhelming.

Keep this receiving box in a room even after you finish organizing it because you will still be organizing other areas and may find new items that belong in this space. You can address these new items in the future when you fine-tune the systems in that room.

> Keep a receiving box in a room even after you finish organizing it because you will still be organizing other areas and may find new items that belong in this space.

Set Up Your Boxes and Bins

Your boxes and bins will be your companions as you organize. These temporary containers will keep your piles separate and clearly labeled so you don't need to revisit your decisions. They are also easy to stack and carry. You will need a minimum of three boxes—keep, donate, dispose—but it's often helpful to have more categories. If possible, have a separate and clearly labeled box or bin for these categories:

☐ **Keep in this room:** You'll know what goes in this box because you've decided on the key purpose or activities for this room. If you think most of the items will stay in the room, after you've made a decision on the item, simply place it right where you found it.

☐ **Keep, but belongs elsewhere in your home:** You can make one box for the entire house or one for upstairs and one for downstairs if you think a lot will be leaving the room. Distribute the contents of this box to receiving boxes in the appropriate rooms only after you've finished organizing for the day.

☐ **Sell**

☐ **Donate:** If possible, have a separate box for each organization you are donating to. It will save you sorting time in the future. At the very least, label each item with where you are donating it so sorting will go faster in the future.

☐ **Give to family or friends:** Again, name each box or put a sticky note on the item.

☐ **Belongs to someone else:** This can include borrowed items and items that belong to someone who no longer lives in the house. It is traumatic, and I'm not overstating this, for someone to throw out your things. I've heard many stories, such as a mother throwing away her daughter's coin collection. The daughter is now in her fifties and still remembers this event; plus, the daughter now tends to hold on to too many things, partly because of this incident. When you are done organizing, you can contact the owners of these items and ask them to come pick them up or offer to ship the items to them.

☐ *Probation box:* This is for items that you can't decide on right now. You may find it easier to make the decision after the room is completely organized.

☐ *Trash/recycle*

Wherever you have space, line up the boxes in the same area. If you keep them all together, you won't need to hunt around the room for the box you are looking for. They all will be side by side, clearly labeled and easy to choose from.

Use these boxes so you don't need to leave the room while you are working. If you leave the area you are working on, you will get sidetracked and may not get back to your main task. Stick with one area until you complete it. Then address the boxes from that area.

WORK LIKE CLOCKWORK

Your holding and receiving areas are ready, as are your boxes. Now you're looking at the room you want to reorganize and wondering where to start. Think clockwork—from left to right. Pick a starting point in the room and work methodically in one direction around the room in a clockwork fashion. This allows you to see progress quickly, which is motivating. The opposite would be crisscrossing the room, or cherry-picking individual items because you know they don't belong in this space. If you use that method, you can't see your progress as clearly.

Imagine a couch that is filled with clothing and other items. Now imagine you've worked on decluttering for a while and can sit down on the couch. What progress! How would that feel? You want the small successes to spur you on and keep you going, particularly when you are starting out, but also when you reach a point when you're just not sure you want to continue. Sometimes that happens.

Work around the perimeter of the room first, working down one wall, then the next. After that's done and you've enjoyed the feeling, work in clockwork fashion on items that are in the middle of the room.

I helped a client transform a dining room into a work/study space. We worked around the perimeter of the room and then worked on one flat surface or in one drawer at a time. When we came to the desk in the middle of the room, we worked on one desk drawer at a time. Then we worked on the items that were standing or sitting next to the desk, around its perimeter. The point is to choose a spot, designate it in your mind, and work only in that spot until you are done. If you need a visual marker, use chalk to outline boundaries on the floor or tabletop. One client came up with her own version of dividing up the space. She had divided her room into quadrants. She would work on one quadrant at a time. Brilliant! She has a strong visual sense, so she could mark off in her mind what belonged in each section she'd work on. Not clockwork, but definitely methodical. Or another client, working on her attic, divided this large space into departments or sections: the home décor area, the memories section, the travel and suitcases area, etc. This is the second *R* of REORGANIZE—round and round. You methodically work around the room while you are organizing.

Pick a starting point in the room and work methodically in one direction around the room in a clockwork fashion. This allows you to see progress quickly, which is motivating.

NO-REGRETS DECISIONS

Now let's talk in more depth about making these tough decisions about what to keep and what to let go of. This is the *G* in REORGA-NIZE—get rid of (or not) and also the *L* in SIMPLIFY—let go without regrets. You may find decision-making is easier because now you really know why you're decluttering or downsizing. The most important thread is why you're doing this. Commitment follows.

The first time you start sorting your belongings, keep the list of questions on pages 101–103 in front of you, along with your completed room tour questions and Home is Not Home Without Chart. When you hold up an object to decide whether to keep it or not, ask yourself those questions.

When deciding what to keep and what to let go of, we all want to make decisions we won't regret. My no-regrets decisions list was inspired by a story my grandmother told me. When my great-grandmother died, my grandmother went to Grammy Nichols' nursing home and got rid of absolutely everything. She didn't save anything. I believe my grandmother's generation was taught to move on quickly, and one way to do that is to pretend as if nothing had ever happened. More than twenty years later, my grandmother would still talk with me about regretting her decision to get rid of everything so quickly in the midst of her grief and sadness.

You may think simplifying and reorganizing will be easier if you just get rid of everything, but convenience now is not worth the regret you will feel later.

You may think simplifying and reorganizing will be easier if you just get rid of everything, but convenience now is not worth the regret you will feel later. That regret may cause you to accumulate more clutter in the future because you are afraid of repeating your mistake. Take your time and fully process your emotions so you can make wise decisions.

You don't need to agonize over every item. If something is trivial and holds no meaning, go ahead and get rid of it. You may indeed throw away something small and then need it a month or so later, but it's easy enough to buy a new one. You made the best decision you knew how to make at the time. It's the major regrets we want to prevent. So start with this list of questions and keep track of which questions resonate and make you think more deeply about your decision. Feel free to write down your own version of no-regrets decisions and list what it would take for you to know that you've made the best decision you can at this time.

- Does this object fit into my new space that I'm imagining—measurements, scale, and style? Don't worry if you are not sure. Some people can visualize their new space, but many cannot. If you're not sure, keep the item for now. If you're thinking it's probably going to leave your house, put it in a probation box.
- Use a scale of 1–10. If it's a 10, it stays; a 1, it goes. Where does this item rank on the scale? Ask yourself this question to know which direction you're leaning. It can help you identify your true feelings for the item.
- Does this item make my house feel more like home? Is it a favorite? Refer to your Home is Not Home Without Chart (page 208).
- Do I love this item? Does anyone else in the family love it? If so, could I give it away, knowing it will have a home with someone I know and respect, who will enjoy the object as I have?
- Has the product expired? If you have lots of books, is the information contained in them out of date now? Science, technology, investment—many categories have information that expires, changes quickly, or can be found easily on the Internet or in a library. Do I already know the information in these magazines? Is there any reason to continue to reference it? Or can I pass along this information to someone who is newer to this topic or field? Many of us gather and keep books, not realizing that we see the bookshelves as proof of how much we know. Think about it and decide whether this is important to you.
- Can I find the information somewhere else (Internet, library, etc.)?
- Do I need the object, or do I just want it to have it?
- Why do I keep this? Say this question out loud and then verbalize your answer. Hear how it sounds. Are you keeping this out of guilt, obligation, and fear? How does that knowledge make you feel about the object? Do you resent it? If so, let go of it. What's the

worst that could happen? This often happens with collections and inherited items. Once people know that you collect a specific item, what happens? Everyone gives you items for your collection. It's as if they stop thinking about what to give you. So in your collection, pick up each individual item and look at it. Why do you keep this one? Is it a true favorite with lots of memories? Or was it simply a gift that you never really had special feelings for? Think, too, about why you started the collection and whether this is still a favorite type of collection. Oftentimes, a collection matches up with a stage of our lives. We continue collecting because people expect it or because they continue our collection by virtue of their gifts. Left alone, we wouldn't keep collecting. If you decide to stop a collection, let those who buy you gifts know so they don't continue to contribute to it.

- How many of these do I really need? Do I need all of these or just a few to remind myself? You can take a picture of each item in your collection (or just take one photo of the entire collection) as a reminder and then give away those that aren't your favorites. This photo idea really works, even for people who call themselves keepers, savers, or sentimental types. People even make a video of themselves, telling the stories of each of the items in the collection. It's a neat way to pass along family stories.

- Would I pay to move it or store it? Sometimes putting a monetary value on a group of items will help, whether you are moving or not.

- If it's a practical item, when did I use it last? If it's more than a year ago, the item probably isn't of real value to you. If you're not using something, then how does it bring joy or value to your life? Couldn't someone else enjoy it more?

- If it's broken, is it worth fixing? How long has this been in the repairs pile? This applies to home repairs, framing of pictures, sewing repairs. Will you really use the item after it is fixed? Or has it been in the fix-it pile because you honestly weren't sure whether you wanted to get it fixed at all?

- Does it fit me and my new lifestyle or the chapter I'm headed into? Give up the corporate suits if you're moving out of that phase. Decide what clothing size you are likely to be. When was the last time your size changed? If you were to change sizes, would the clothes you have still be in style when you are able to wear them again?
- Does the good money spent on the item outweigh the space it takes up? Clothing, tools, and dinnerware—many items fall in this category because they've become part of the scenery of our home. If you're not enjoying the item, then you're not getting your money's worth anyway, so who else would help you make sure its value is realized? Plus, you'll experience an emotional payback in this way, another kind of value. Consider selling the item to recoup some of what you spent on it.
- Will you really get to this project you've been saving? Someday is today. You're all about moving on now, so this is a great time to make a decision about all those projects you've bought the materials for. In the context of your new chapter and how you hope to spend your time, will you do this particular project or not?
- If it's a gift you never enjoyed, can you pass it along as a gift to someone else? Unless they gave you the gift, they'll never know if you regift it!
- Do I want my children to have this? Do I want them to go through all of this stuff? Realize that the decisions you don't make will eventually need to be made by someone else. This knowledge is a powerful motivator for some people.
- Would I buy it again?
- What organization would appreciate and need this more than I do?

No-Regrets Decisions for Inherited Items

How can you make sure not to dishonor the legacy of a person when getting rid of items? This is a key question I'm asked when I work with a client on organizing inherited items, items given to them by an older relative during his or her lifetime, or items from a close family member, spouse, or partner who has died. It seems that if you throw away all the things he or she gave you, you're disrespecting family history or the person, or denying the person ever existed.

When we're overwhelmed or momentarily caught up in the emotion and grief, we sometimes think in an all-or-nothing, black-and-white way. Don't make decisions when you are still in this stage.

As you evaluate the items, ask yourself, what was the essence of this person? What was he all about? What were his values? What was his personality? What is his legacy that you'd like to pass on?

When you can define the essence of the person, you have reached a place where you can keep enough to honor the person and to help you with memories. If you can't do this yet, then you haven't processed that initial grief; you're more interested in keeping everything so you have constant reminders around you. Wait until you can identify the person's essence and then go through things in stages as your grief eventually turns into acceptance. You needn't keep everything the person owned to keep alive the legacy, memories, and the essence of the person.

Consider using a memory box to help set parameters for how much you keep. You can buy a box or use something around the house that fits the person's style and personality. One woman has one memory box for her husband and another memory box for her mother. Both are on the top shelf of her closet, so she sees them every day.

Answer the Questions With Others

If you find that you're still keeping too much, then stop for the day. Either come back to it the next day or call someone to work with you—a friend or a professional. A few years after my divorce, I realized I hadn't touched any of my needlework or handcrafts, so I thought my handcrafting days were over. I had just started working as a professional organizer and thought it would be easy for me to go through these items, get rid of what I didn't want or need, and reorganize the rest. I spent an hour. I kept everything! Well, except a few items that had gone bad.

I stopped. I called a friend, gave her the printed list of questions, and asked her to ask me those questions out loud as she sat beside me. The more I went through things, the more I talked, the more I understood the connection. I explained to my friend that I had grown up as the creative one in the family. Needlework is a skill that my grandmother taught me when she spent a lot of time at my house while I was growing up. I had also done a lot of needlework while I was married. My conversation helped me see all of my emotional connections to my crafts—they were a part of my identity in my family, a legacy from my grandmother, and a part of my marriage. I realized my supplies represented more than just "stuff." I realized I had kept everything because subconsciously I had placed a lot of emotional value on the supplies. With this understanding, I was able to disconnect my identity and heritage from every single craft item and select only my favorites and what I would truly use. I whittled down my crafts by more than half without any regrets.

Talking with a friend helped me because I am a verbal processor. If you are a verbal processor, find a friend who will listen and not judge. If you are an internal processor, spend some time alone and really reflect on your feelings toward the objects you can't let go of. Write out your feelings if that will help you process.

> When we're overwhelmed or momentarily caught up in the emotion and grief, we sometimes think in an all-or-nothing, black-and-white way. Don't make decisions when you are still in this stage.

Making No-Regrets Decisions on Valuable Items

Before you sell or give away anything, you'll want to decide or find out the value of what you're getting rid of first. This is another part of having no-regrets decisions. By value, I do mean financial, but also sentimental and historical. You don't need to keep any item simply because it is valuable. Knowing the value of an item will simply help you pass the item on in the most fitting way. Valuable items can be sold sentimental objects can be given to loved ones; historical items can go to museums, collections, or historical societies.

THE MORE YOU PURGE, THE EASIER IT GETS

As you start on your first organizing project, understand that your tolerance for "stuff" will decline as you work on each space. You may find that you need to return to fine-tune the organization in certain places—either because

> "People have unique perceptions of that crossover point when possessions become clutter."
>
> – LINDA SAMUELS, CPO-CD®

it turned out to be too hard to tackle on that day you had devoted to it, or because you want to get rid of more. One phrase I often use with clients is to focus on "progress, not perfection." Start with what feels comfortable and know you can always come back later.

If you're in a room with sentimental objects, this room will be emotionally tiring for you to work on, though perhaps not physically tiring. This is when you'll really want to think about whether you work alone or with someone in the room. Recognize this will happen and stop earlier than you typically would so you don't get burned-out. Let your mind and heart relax a bit and then continue. There's a lot going on in your mind as you do this.

Sometimes it will feel like you are just moving stuff around. But you have to start somewhere. The reorganizing and decluttering process is like doing a puzzle. Just as with a puzzle, you'll group like pieces together and then move them to where they belong. That creates more space for the next group of pieces you want to work in the puzzle or the next set of stuff or piles in your organizing space. We have to remove pieces that don't belong in a space to make room for the transformation.

KEEPING TRACK OF WHERE YOU ARE AND OF DECISIONS

After you finish your organizing work for the day, you may want to make an inventory of all the items you are giving away and selling. This list will record your decisions and can support getting a tax deduction. It can also help you ensure you are giving equally among family members. The inventory can be a handwritten list, a spreadsheet, photographs of key items, or a video of each room—whatever makes you feel comfortable. You can use software to complete an entire home inventory if you want to have something more elaborate. Quicken has home inventory software. The Insurance Information Institute does as well. Or you can make up your own with information you think is important. Don't spend so much time creating your list that you stop the actual reorganizing decisions, though.

A record can also be accomplished by putting removable stickers on each piece of furniture (or tags, pinned to the back of items so the tags are out of sight). On the sticker, you can write who the item is for or write the history or story of items. This method inspires some people. I worked with a woman who was moving on after a divorce. She called because she was overwhelmed, not sure where to start, and thought she had not made much progress on her own. When we put stickers and tags on items she had made decisions about, she couldn't believe how much progress she'd already made. She had been keeping it in all in her head, but seeing the stickers and tags gave her a clear picture of her progress, and it inspired her to continue.

DEALING WITH ITEMS LEAVING YOUR HOME

Congratulations. The hard part is over—all those decisions have been made. You now have boxes of items that are leaving your home. We need to do something with those boxes before we can put your room back together. As I said earlier, a general guideline for getting items out of your house is to put the boxes into your car right away. Put them in the trunk. And so you don't forget about them, write yourself a note on an errands pad you keep in the front seat near the dashboard. Remind yourself to stop at your donation or consignment places. If you need a longer distance trip or your schedule is busy, write yourself a note in your calendar. Figure out when you'll be in the area of the store or donation site, and make an appointment. All these steps will prevent the boxes from overstaying their welcome in your trunk.

Items That Belong to Someone Else

If you have adult children who no longer live with you, you probably have lots of their belongings still in your house, particularly in their old bedrooms. I'm often asked how to get adult children to remove their stuff from their parents' home. What is true in this situation is that children often have forgotten what they've left at their parents' house. You see the items in their rooms often because you live with the items. My mother and I speculate that leaving things at home is the child's way of hanging on to their family home. Others have said that when a child moves out, their first home or apartment is typically smaller than the family home, so they keep things at their parents' purely for storage, and then they simply forget what they've left there.

> Don't get rid of anything that is not yours to make a decision about. The best approach is to list all of the items that belong to your children that are still in your home and send them the list.

As I've said before, don't get rid of anything that is not yours to make a decision about. The best approach is to list all of the items that belong to your children that are still in your home and send them the list. Ask them to identify the things they know without a doubt they don't want, and get their permission to get rid of these things. Then you can ask them to take away everything that's left the next time they visit. Or you can wait until they visit and ask them to go through all the items and take the ones they want to keep, with the understanding that you will get rid of whatever is left. If you have a lot of artwork and schoolwork, winnow it down to the best items and give it to your child as a present, with the understanding that they may not want to keep all of it. My mother did this for me. I looked through my box, and out of a nearly two-foot pile of papers, I saved about ten items as memories. Even though I kept few items, the experience of going through the others was a sentimental journey into my past, which I enjoyed. When I finished reviewing everything, the journey was done, and I didn't feel the need to keep everything I'd been given, just the special ones I might pull out again someday.

How to Give to Family and Friends

When you worked around your room, you had a box for items you wanted to give to family or friends. I suggest giving away those items first, because the feeling you'll have when you see their faces or hear their joy will make all this work worth it. Here are some examples of how you can present items to loved ones in a fun, fair, and stress-free way.

Have a party. Some people will have parties or gatherings to give away items. One client had a clothing party with all her sisters after she organized her closet. Another client had a family gathering. The client was helping her mother empty her apartment so her mother could live with my client. The client's siblings were called in, partly to help Mom get settled at my client's home, but also to have a family gathering. Mom settled in her chair and told stories about many of the items she was giving to her children.

For several years, my grandmother gave us gifts from her past chapter with my step-grandfather, Uncle Dick. We cherished the gifts and the stories she told with them. Sometime after Uncle Dick died, she gave me an "I love you" ring he'd given her prior to their marriage. It happened to be around the time I was getting divorced, so it was even more comforting than she may have realized for me to wear a new ring on my left hand. She was moving on, as was I.

Let family members choose. Another benefit of having a gathering is that family members can choose which items they want, which is one less decision you need to make. There are several ways to make this process fair. Some families draw straws. They go around in a circle and each person gets to choose one item. Your turn is based on the length of your straw. If there are items two people want, they figure it out; no stress for the giver.

Divide it evenly. Some people will use their decisions record, including financial values on the items, to be sure that family members get their equal share of items, based on financial value.

Sell Items

Before you sell anything, have items you think have significant monetary valuable appraised. Experts at consignment shops, auctioneers, eBay resellers, and antique dealers can help with appraisal. Always get at least two estimates, just as you would with a home renovation project. Ask your friends and colleagues if they have sold objects. Just as you would if you were renovating your home or looking for a new doctor, find a trusted, recommended local resource. You're letting go of items you once loved, so if you have a trusted resource, this letting-go process becomes easier. There are many options available when it comes to selling—estate sales, garage sales, online sites, and consignment shop.

Estate sales. If you have a lot of items to remove, including furniture, contact local estate sales people, also called estate liquidators. Despite the professional title, you don't need to be wealthy to have an estate sale. The word is more often used to signify that the bulk of your belongings will be on sale. Don't worry if you think you don't have enough items. These companies sometimes combine property from two or more houses to have one larger sale.

Estate sales people work like consignment shops. Because they are doing the marketing, selling, and moving of your former belongings, they deserve to be paid, so they take a percentage of what you earn from the sale.

Consignment shops. Consignment can be a good option if you have a few high-end items to sell. Shops will want to see pictures or the items themselves to assess their sales value. Some consignment shops will donate your items if not sold, or you can take them back if you want them. However, I wouldn't advise taking back an item that didn't sell; you've made the difficult decision to let the item go, so taking it back would be emotionally difficult. Stick to your decisions.

Beware of garage sales because you make little money for the time you invest. And if you're removing things you once loved from your home, it's emotionally difficult to negotiate prices with people on these items.

EBay resellers. You can create an eBay account of your own and sell the item yourself, or you can hire someone to do this for you. If you choose to hire someone, your best bet is to find a person whom a friend has hired, but you can also look on the Internet for a local reseller or a group that can recommend one of their members. The benefit of eBay is that your items will be viewed beyond just your local geographic area. Selling on eBay takes time and expertise. Decide whether you want to use a reseller who will take a percentage or whether you want to use your time this way. You may have already sold items online or have a friend or family member who does, so that's a good option, too.

Garage sales. I'm not a big fan of garage sales because you make little money for the time you invest. And if you're removing things you once loved from your home, it's emotionally difficult to negotiate price, with people on these items. Neighborhood yard sales are easier. Or check your local Scout troops, churches, and boys and girls clubs for dates for their annual rummage sales. These community sales have a built-in audience, potentially larger than an individual sale would attract.

Craigslist: Craigslist is a way to advertise your items online to a local audience. If you use this option, meet the person buying your item in a public place, such as a library, and don't meet the person alone. This is a good safety precaution. Set a deadline for how long you will post the item and put the deadline in the listing so people make faster decisions if they want to buy.

Selling your items on your own can be quite time-consuming. If you are contemplating this option, ask yourself these questions:

- How much time can I devote to selling these items? You probably don't want this to become a part-time job, so be realistic.
- Will the amount of money I make be worth the effort it takes to sell the items? Items appraised for a high price are worth selling, but in reality, your everyday items don't fetch as high a price as you'd hope.
- What are your feelings about privacy? Are you comfortable meeting people or having them come to your home to look at the things you are selling?

When it comes to selling everyday items, remember we attach emotion to the objects we own, even if they were once favorites and are no more. For example, you may have bought a gorgeous plate on your honeymoon trip. Wonderful stories about it abound, and that's the value to you. The financial value to someone who could buy the plate, however, will be less.

If it's going to be difficult for you to hear what the financial value is of a once-cherished object, don't sell the item yourself. Have a family member, friend, or business person sell the item for you. You've done the hard work; enjoy it without worries. Let it go so you can move on. Some people feel like they've finished the hard part—the decisions—so they don't want to extend this process by going to myriad stores and organizations to drop off their belongings.

Depending on what age or stage of your life you're in, you may also find that objects you were saving cannot be used any longer. Car child safety seats are a clear example. The safety regulations have changed several times just in the past few years. With each change, there are seats that can no longer be sold. You may find, too, that certain types of objects are not in use the way they used to be. Silver and china dishes are two examples in my lifetime. It seems fewer brides are requesting these items, and yet our mothers and grandmothers expected they would pass down these items. The next generation will view some of your belongings in a different light and will not value them in the same way as you do.

Where to Donate

After you've given items to family and friends and sold items, you're ready to donate what's left. As I mentioned in chapter four, having a great place to donate your items can motivate you to give more items away. Think about who would be interested in the items you have. One woman I worked with had some rug hooking frames she made rugs on. We called the state council of arts and asked for their ideas. They gave us names of teachers of rug hooking who loved the donated equipment. Magazines, books, and even encyclopedias can go to nursing homes. Handmade doilies went to a senior center; people who shop there are of an age where they use doilies on their bureaus and

When you think of places to donate, think of organizations that could benefit the most from your items. Think of groups that support your values or that have enriched your life or the lives of your loved ones.

their tables. Empty CD jewel cases were donated to a photographer who takes photos of returning soldiers and sends CDs of the photos to their families.

Talk to the organizations you are part of, friends, and local store owners. It's a creative and fun process to find new homes for your things if you want to distribute them this way.

Joy's husband had suddenly passed away several years before she hired me to help her make her house her own. During my first visit, she told me her husband's books would be the last we'd go through. Her husband loved his books, and they represented his essence to Joy, so they carried a lot of emotion for her. The books were not about topics she enjoyed, so the next time she went to the library, she brought in a list of some of his books. The library wanted all the titles, either for the stacks or to support a fundraiser. It was easier for Joy to remove the books from her house because she could imagine a young person reading her husband's books and enjoying learning as he had.

Another client, Christine, made beautiful greeting cards from exquisite papers and embellishments. She wanted to add a new craft to her crafting space but had run out of room, so she needed to cull her collection. A relative Christine had cared for had a wonderful experience at an Alzheimer's day-away program. There were several such programs in Christine's area. We contacted them to see if Christine's craft items would be of interest. Schools, religious organizations, career centers, caregiving facilities, homeless shelters, and animal shelters are all wonderful options.

They were, so Christine made the trip to the program, met the staff and some of the clients, and gave her gifts. Imagine how good that felt.

When you think of places to donate, think of organizations that could benefit the most from your items. Think of groups that support your values or that have enriched your life or the lives of your loved ones, as Christine's story illustrates. Be creative. Schools, religious organizations, career centers, caregiving facilities, hospitals, battered women's shelters, foster care facilities, homeless shelters, and animal shelters are all wonderful options. Give them a call, describe your donation, and see if they would like to receive it.

TAKEAWAY POINTS
Work around the room like clockwork, making no-regrets decisions as you go. Stay in this one room for as long as you've designated to organize—it could be thirty minutes, an hour, or an afternoon. The main point is to stay focused. Continue working in this manner until you have gone through every item in the room. It may take you several organizing sessions to do this, but that's okay. You need to remove everything that you don't want to keep before you can reorganize the items you do keep. Don't get in a rush to start rearranging. In the next chapter we'll organize the items you decided to keep by wrapping up the remaining letters in REORGANIZE: analyze remaining items; negotiate the space versus your belongings; implement; zebra, be one; and evaluate, evaluate.

7. Reorganizing What's Left

CONGRATULATIONS ON MAKING IT THIS FAR! You've finished the hard part—deciding what to let go of. Now it's on to the fun part—reorganizing what's left so you get the most out of your belongings and your home. In this chapter, we'll finish the REORGANIZE process and explore the *A*, *N*, *I*, *Z*, and *E* steps. These principles will help you create organizing systems that work for you so you feel great about every part of your home. We'll also explore the *I* and *F* in SIMPLIFY. I'll give you practical examples of these concepts to guide you and inspire you in your own home.

ENVISION YOUR NEW SPACE

In chapter five you toured your home and asked yourself specific questions in each room. Now that you've removed unwanted items from your home, it's time to tour the new, clutter-free rooms and revisit the room tour questions (see page 206) and your answers to them.

Your answers to each question will help you move forward and reorganize the space. They will also set you up for success by helping you identify systems that work and systems that don't work for you in this space. Let's look at a few of the questions in a little more detail to help you envision your new space.

What Activities Would You Like to Have Happen Here?

You removed the clutter that was preventing you from using this room as you wanted. Now you can focus on transforming the room into the space you want it to be. Will you return the room to the same purpose it had before you began your reorganizing project, or would you like to reinvent the space? Are there activities you do somewhere else in the house that you'd like to give more space to or a more convenient space? Could any of those activities occur here, in this room?

By identifying the activities that will occur in the room, you are identifying the function of the room. Survey the current contents of the room. Does everything in it serve the function of the room?

Do you have new responsibilities or activities that you need to accommodate? Maybe your mother has moved in with you and needs space somewhere to store her daily medications. Or perhaps you've gone back to school and you need to make a space for studying and writing. Write these down and decide how you need to arrange the room to best facilitate these activities. You'll find specific ideas for repurposing rooms later in the chapter.

Does Anything Need to be Added to This Space to Fulfill its Function?

By identifying the activities that will occur in the room, you are identifying the function of the room. Survey the current contents of the room. Does everything in it serve the function of the room? Do you need to add items to the room to better serve its function?

Do you need to improve lighting, move furniture, or combine similar items from another room. Now is your chance to consolidate. For example, if clearing a closet opened up extra space, you may be able to store your off-season clothing in the closet instead of storing it somewhere else.

ANALYZE THE REMAINING ITEMS

Now that you've re-envisioned the room, you can analyze the remaining items (those staying in the room) and decide how to organize them.

Like With Like

One of the most basic principles of organizing is to keep "like" or similar things together.

Visualize how a store is laid out, or notice it the next time you're there. At each store, the goods are organized in similar groups, and the groups are located in specific aisles or sections of the store, which makes it easy to find what you are looking for. When you shop at these stores, it's easy enough to find the items you purchase often, isn't it?

When you combine like items, you are creating the sections or aisles in your room or area. Analyze each item you have in the room and put similar items together in different piles. Don't worry about where you will put them yet; simply create your groupings.

Like with like can also mean grouping items you often use together. An example in the garage would be if you hang the weed trimmer on a nail, and on the same nail, you hang the instruction manual enclosed in a plastic bag or sheet protector. One is a tool and one is paper instructions, but they are always used together. Or in the bathroom you may group together all of the grooming products you use on a daily basis, even though it may include a wide variety of items. Extra or less frequently used items would go in different groups.

A common mistake: Don't forget the "absent items."

Quantify the Size of Your Groups

After you create your groups of like items, measure and count each group. Record these measurements in a notepad, as they will help you negotiate the space and find homes for everything. Be sure to account for any

Consolidate ... or Not?

Some people want to keep all like things together in one central location, while others like to keep things where they are used. Towels and linens are good examples of what to consolidate, or not. You could have a central linen closet where all of the towels and linens in the house are located, or you could spread the towels out and keep sets in each bathroom and keep sheets in bedroom closets. Everyone is different, and there's no right or wrong choice. Most important is to choose a grouping that you can remember and easily maintain.

missing items—that is, items that are in the laundry or in the dishwasher, books in another room, or other like items spread across the house. If, for example, you know you will be keeping all of your board games in this area, but you know you have games spread around the house, take the time to round up all the games and add them to your pile so you can find the right-sized home for them.

Plan for growth. As you quantify each group, decide if the number of items in the group will grow in the future. I know, we're in the middle of decluttering, and now I'm suggesting you add to your collection. Why do I do this? Because sometimes you get rid of old collections, hobbies, or clothing with the idea of replacing them with new collections, hobbies, or clothing. You may not take up the entire space that has just been vacated by its former tenants, but part of transition organizing is welcoming the new while removing the old. So plan for new needs. Write down your plans so you know how much extra space you need to leave for this group so you can properly display or store the items. You can also use a placeholder. For example, you're making your room into a place to make jewelry. Currently, some beads are in another room. On a sheet of paper, in big letters, write "beads from the dining room" (if that's where they are now). Put the placeholder paper in the room you're reorganizing, in the spot you plan to house the beads (or any other object).

NEGOTIATE THE SPACE VERSUS YOUR BELONGINGS

After you analyze the remaining items, find homes for them in the room. This is the *N* in REORGANIZE—negotiate the space versus your belongings. Look at and measure each group of items. Now look around the room. This is the space you have to work with. Will each group fit into the space you want it to fit? Draw a diagram if you'd like, or start moving things around. If the group doesn't fit, try another spot. Belongings often end up on a miscellaneous shelf because we don't leave enough space for them. We put the items where they fit, for now, thinking we'll get back to them. Over time, if you don't organize as you add or take away items on that shelf, you get a jumbled collection of items that don't belong together. Your likes are no longer together, and you'll have multiple places to hunt for items. That's why it's important quantify and measure your belongings before you assign items to a new home within the room.

Look around the room and identify a specific home for each group of like items. Put frequently used items in your everyday space within the room.

Identify Your Everyday Space

Everyday space is often a new concept for people I work with. The idea is to keep your everyday living spaces—those that you spend the most time in—comfortable, easy to maintain, and filled with the belongings you use on a daily, or near daily, basis. The space is filled with belongings that are appealing to you—visually, energetically, and intuitively. Think about how often you use the things you own. You can live more simply, reorganize less often, and maintain more easily if you have less stuff around you day to day.

Identify the items you use daily. These items should be placed where they are easy to access and easy to put away. Tabletops and flat surfaces, shelves and drawers within arm's reach, and floor space are all prime real estate—the easiest-to-access areas of your room. Keep everyday items on shelves or drawers that don't require bending or reaching. You may need to recategorize some items to put them in these prime spots.

Everyday space: Where you spend the most time, or the space you use almost daily, which you would like to be clutter-free. This is the prime real estate of your home.

Examples of items to keep in everyday space include:

- Books you're currently reading or plan to read
- Utensils you use most often
- Files you use most often

In your clothes closet, the spaces that are easy to see and access when you first open the door are your everyday space. Keep clothing you don't wear as often in less accessible spaces such as high rods or the top shelves.

Consider Your Shelving and Container Needs

As you identify new homes for everything in your room, you may find you need to bring in additional shelving or containers. You can buy new shelves and containers, or you can "shop" around your home and use items you already have. Take three-dimensional measurements (height, depth, and width) of the space the container or shelf has to fit into *before going shopping*. We've all done this, right? The container won't fit the stuff, or it won't fit into the space. We eyeball the space, but few of us are accurate this way. So we don't make the best use of the space. And if we're wrong, we've just wasted time we really didn't have!

A Few Notes on Buying Products

Beyond measuring your groups and finding containers to fit each group, here are some recommendations for purchasing shelving and containers.

- It is tempting to shop for products at the beginning of your project. Please don't. You'll waste time and money. For most reorganizing projects, you'll want to know what each container needs to do for you, what it needs to hold. Some people buy the largest-sized bins, not knowing what they need to store. The problem with large bins is that you end up with piles inside the bins. The bins are too large, so items swim in them and it's still hard to find what you want.

- Try using clear containers when it's feasible and attractive. Clear means you (and those around you) can see what's in the bins, and, therefore, which similar items belong there—and which do not! Clear bins can eliminate the need for labels, although I maintain labelling makes it easier to find and retrieve items.

- Open or covered: Everyone has a preference here, and often it's a preference based on the room or what's being stored. Visual clutter can be distracting and scramble your thoughts. It can also be an energy drain. Lids keep clutter out of sight. The advantage to open bins is that it's easier to put things away. You eliminate the step of taking off the lid. It sounds simple, but in some homes, this makes a big difference.

- When you shop in your house or at stores for organizing containers, be creative in how you use containers. Just because you need a box in your office to hold small paper receipts does not mean you have to buy a product from the "office" section at your favorite organization store. Think about what the container needs to do for you, how it needs to function, and its characteristics. Then look at organizing products for other rooms, or look at items you have at home that seem to be decorative only, but could find a new purpose in life. You'll be more excited about

using a container or organizing product if you enjoy it. Use or buy products you find both functional and appealing.

- Spend more on organizing products that you will use most often—those that will contain items you use most often. Spend less on organization that will be hidden away. Again, the idea is that you will be more likely to use organizing containers you enjoy. If you have two products that will serve the same purpose, buy the one you like best, even if it's more money, if you will use it every day or every week. You'll get your money's worth by using it more and maintaining your clutter-free environment.

Have a specific idea of what you want before you bring a shelf or container into your home. Identify what exactly you will be storing in it or on it. If you are putting bins on shelves, measure the space between the shelves (the height, top to bottom) and measure the bins with the lids on. Sometimes the manufacturer's labels are for the bin itself, but if your shelf space is tight, you might buy the wrong size because the lid actually extends beyond the edges of the bin. When you look at shelving, calculate how many bins can fit onto each shelf so you know if all the bins you need will fit. Measure the height of the shelves, both for the entire set and also from shelf to shelf. Also measure the width of the shelves, so you know how many bins can fit across. Your best bet is always to buy adjustable shelving. Plan for growth and items you've lent out or forgotten about.

IMPLEMENT

You've got your groups of like items together. You've identified your storage needs and made necessary additions (whether store-bought or moved from another room in the house). Now you can implement your new systems in each area, one section at a time. This is the *I* in REORGA-NIZE. It's also the *I* in SIMPLIFY. Simply carry out your plan. Arrange the items around the room in a way that is logical to you and best serves the functions of the room. Keep your everyday space in mind and place frequently used items with maximum convenience in mind.

You may want or need to move furniture around before you place your items back in the room. See which layout makes you feel productive or inspired or comfortable. You can buy furniture-mover disks at office supply stores to help you move large or heavy items. The disks have a smooth side that goes on the floor and a foam side that sticks to the bottom of the furniture. For wood floors, put a sock over each disk. It requires a little effort to get your furniture onto the slides, but after that, you can move a big piece of furniture with just a finger or two.

Working With a Professional Organizer

If you decide to work with a professional organizer, interview organizers with each of the certifications I've listed here: Certified Professional Organizer ® (CPO), Certified Professional Organizer in Chronic Disorganization® (CPO-CD), and Certified Organizer Coach®. It's crucial that you feel there is a fit with the organizer and his or her specialties; the organizer's experience is key to successful reorganization. You want someone with experience so you can tailor your organizing systems to your situation and issues. The CPO® is the basic certification for organizers. The specialty in CD is for people who have a chronic issue with disorganization.* And the Certified Organizer Coach® may or may not work alongside you in the home; some work with you by phone in combination with side-by-side assistance, and others work mainly by phone.

*The Institute for Challenging Disorganization has many fact sheets available to the public. If you have an ongoing issue with disorganization, you may be chronically disorganized and need the specialized support of the organizer with this specialty, the CPO-CD®. Chronic disorganization is defined this way by the ICD on its website: Chronic disorganization is having a past history of disorganization in which self-help efforts to change have failed, an undermining of current quality of life due to disorganization, and the expectation of future disorganization.

One Area at a Time

Most people find it less overwhelming to organize by area instead of looking at the room as a whole. And by dividing up your space, mentally or on a diagram, you can work on reorganizing in small bits of time so the project fits into your schedule. You'll get one section completely done at a time, which will motivate you to get back into the space to work on the next section.

If one section still seems overwhelming, here are a few ideas to get you started. They may or may not be the way you continue to work on your organizing. Remember, the hardest part—identifying items that are leaving your home—is over. Now you are simply re-creating the space with all of the items you love and use. Putting the room back together will be a very positive experience.

- Use your timer so you work for only a short time, such as fifteen or thirty minutes.
- Break down sections into smaller parts and work on only one part at a time. A smaller part could be a drawer, a shelf, a stack, or a pile.
- Bring your audio book or your music. Organize for two songs or for a chapter.
- Work side-by-side with a friend or Certified Professional Organizer (CPO)® or a CPO-CD®. (The CD means they are certified in working with people who are chronically disorganized.) They can assist you in getting started, staying motivated, finishing up, and even maintaining. Use the talents of outside professionals for the most difficult parts so you don't get stuck and give up.
- Work with a Certified Organizer Coach® by phone. Hiring a coach, my clients tell me, is like hiring a personal trainer.
- Decide what your reward will be before you get started.

Here are a couple of additional points to consider as you implement your organizing systems.

Use organizing containers even on shelves. Containers keep like items together, which makes it easier to find what you need. My general guideline is once you have two of a similar type of item, find a bin, basket, or other container for them. Loose items on shelves are like papers. Over time, they seem to melt and merge together. You can also make more efficient use of the height of each shelf by using taller or stackable containers.

Label your containers. This helps you remember where each item belongs and lets you find items quickly without looking in each container. The labels don't need to be boring. There are many ways to make fun labels—be as creative as you want! Make your own, search online for label templates, or buy a label maker. Once you start, you'll find yourself labeling all around your house. Labels will also help other members of your household understand your new system. Labels allow you to easily delegate. You can say, "Go put this away in the bin labelled 'games' in your room." One client labelled her pantry so when friends helped cook, they could easily find what they needed on their own. I like to say that labels are the brain's final way to remind you that you are about to put something where it does not belong!

> Containers keep like items together, which makes it easier to find what you need. You can also make more efficient use of the height of each shelf by using taller or stackable containers.

Remember the Three Ps: As you organize your room and your belongings, identify the people, process, and products you need to have a functioning system. Set up your system so that each *P* is accounted for. Imagine people using the organizing system you've created, or ask them about it. Is the system easy to use? Simple but effective? Easy to remember? Does it take advantage of habits they already have? Too much change all at once is difficult, so remember to keep it simple, effective, and easy to maintain. See chapter three for a review of this concept.

ZEBRA! BE ONE

You may be panicked that this book doesn't tell you where to specifically place every one of your belongings. Organizing isn't about following someone else's plans or directions. It's about finding what works for you. Just as each zebra has a unique set of stripes, each human has a different way of thinking and organizing. Your organizing solution is unique to how you live and work. That's why zebra is the *Z* in REORGANIZE. Your system has to be specifically tailored to you for it to work. Try out your new space. See how it works for a few weeks. Try out a few changes at a time, get them solidified as habits, and then try out other changes. This gradual approach gives you a better chance at adoption.

Most important, don't compare your organizing systems to others, and don't hold yourself to an unrealistic standard. Your home doesn't need to be magazine-worthy to be organized. Embrace your uniqueness.

If you're still looking for more ideas, see the Room-by-Room section in this chapter.

EVALUATE, EVALUATE, AND FINE-TUNE YOUR IDEAS

Organizing is an ongoing process. Organizing systems require constant use and maintenance to be effective. Hopefully you've created systems that are easy and natural for you to use so they simply become habits and you give them very little thought. However, you'll stay on track with your organizing if you continually evaluate your systems. After you've given yourself enough time to solidify the system and create new habits (about a month), ask yourself, "Am I satisfied with how this works?" If you find something isn't working, ask yourself what has changed. You may discover you are experiencing another life transition and need to adapt to new circumstances. Review

> Organizing is an ongoing process. Organizing systems require constant use and maintenance to be effective.

the Three Ps in the system to identify what specifically isn't working and find a solution. This is how you fine-tune your organizing systems—the F in SIMPLIFY.

If you go through another major life event, evaluate how your current systems must change. What works for you in one stage will change as you move on to another stage.

TEACHING OTHERS YOUR SYSTEM

You have two more tasks after you finish reorganizing a room. First, let everyone you live with know where things go. You've just made some changes, and if you want to keep things organized, everyone needs to be educated to support the system going forward.

Labels will help the people you live with follow the new system. Praise them when they follow the system, and offer immediate, gentle correction when they don't. Everyone forgets, especially when something is new. If the system still isn't working, redesign it with their input so they can use it effectively. Habits can take twenty-one times in use—so at least three weeks—to get ingrained, longer if you have a brain-based challenge (ADHD, traumatic brain injury, etc.). So give it enough time to become routine.

The second task is maintenance. Some people pick up as they go, putting things away as soon as they're finished using them. Other people are more comfortable with doing a big sweep, either at the end of the day or, sometimes, at the end of the week. This is a personal decision: How much clutter can you live with before you have to clear it? How does clutter get in your way, especially as you create your next chapter? And how much clutter will make you give up on your system? It's much easier to pick up a day's worth of items than a week's worth. If you can't do daily, aim for every other day so piles are manageable and quickly put away. Don't beat yourself up about it. Do keep track of what gets in your way, what takes you off track, and how you get back on course.

ROOM-BY-ROOM REORGANIZING IDEAS

Your answers to the room tour questions, the Home is Not Home Without Chart, and the strategies in this chapter will help you organize your rooms just the way you want them. For additional inspiration, this section offers room-specific ideas for putting it all back together.

Entryway to Your Home

I worked with a client who had separated from her husband and moved into a new home. She called because the space in her new home was so different from her old home that she needed assistance figuring out how to adapt her systems to her new home.

Her new entryway was much smaller than her old one, but she still wanted to fit all of the activities that had gone on in her old entryway into her new entryway without changing anything. Because there was no closet in the entryway of the new home, we had to find new homes for everything she stored in her previous closet, which included coats for all seasons and sports equipment. We started by separating the coats by season and then purchasing a coatrack to hold current-season coats in the entryway. My client selected a rack that matched the décor of her new home as a reward for her organizing efforts. We found storage spaces for off-season coats and sports equipment in other areas of the house.

My client had an effective routine in place for reviewing the day with her children. In the old house this routine had taken place in the entryway, but the new entry was too small. Because the system was so established, it really required only minor adjustments. The only thing that changed was instead of stopping in this smaller entryway, her children would keep walking ten more steps to the kitchen table and go through the routine there. We tried several ideas before landing on her best solution for dealing with paperwork and mail (which was something she used to do in her entryway). We tried looking for a specific-sized table for the front hall for papers, but we couldn't find one. And then it would have been too far away from the kids and the discussions at the table. We thought about moving all of this to the living room, but the kids had snacks when they came home, so the kitchen was the most logical spot. We tried a file holder she loved and had used at her old house, but it was too big for her new kitchen. And she also realized she didn't want an open organizer in her everyday living space. She thought about using a cupboard to keep papers behind doors, but the space wouldn't allow it. Her latest solution is that current papers are kept in folders in a drawer in the kitchen. As the folders or drawer get crowded, she cycles out papers by filing them in a more permanent place. She takes them up with her at the end of the day or end of the week to be filed away in the home office, which has the household files, too. Sometimes you have to live with your first idea, try it out, and figure out what works or doesn't work about it. Sometimes it can be hard to let go of what used to work, especially if you felt like it was the ideal solution. But life events, time, and space change things.

Reorganizing Now-Spare Bedrooms

Hopefully you've respectfully removed your grown children's belongings from their old bedrooms, giving them an opportunity go through what they'd left at home and to keep items or get rid of them. This space is now yours to reinvent. It can still contain a bed for overnight guests, if you wish, but make this room part of your everyday space. Here are some examples to get you thinking creatively about how you could use this new space.

A new home office and study space. One of my clients was a widow who was returning to school in her sixties. She decided to use one of her spare bedrooms as a study space and office to manage household duties previously handled by her husband.

A spare bedroom is now yours to reinvent. It can still contain a bed for overnight guests, if you wish, but make this room part of your everyday space.

She identified all the things she would need for her study space: a desk with space to write at and for a computer, a shelf near the desk for textbooks, and a space to spread out in when she had projects.

We ended up arranging a desk, shelf, and table in an L shape so she could access the desk, table, and shelf without leaving her chair.

She also identified everything she would need to manage her household: a calendar to schedule maintenance calls and keep track of bill due dates and a filing system for bills to pay, paid bills, and tax records. We incorporated these items into the room. It's much easier and faster to reorganize if you begin with your list of needs.

A room for someone new. Perhaps you are on the other end of the spectrum, and you are welcoming a baby or a foster child into your home. If you were previously using the spare bedroom as an office, craft, or activity room, you'll need to find a new location for these activities and set up the room to meet the needs of your new household member. Or perhaps your aging parent is moving in with you so you can better care for their physical needs. You'll need to make room for your parent's belongings and relinquish this space entirely to them so they can enjoy some privacy and independence.

One of my clients hosted a soccer player each summer, which meant some reorganizing and winnowing out. It was such a wonderful and generous use of her extra space. And the arrival of the soccer player was a good example of a manufactured deadline for reorganizing!

Master Bedroom

As you reorganize your bedroom, remember the concept of everyday space. This entire room is everyday space, so only keep things that you use regularly and enjoy in this space. If you do store items here, designate the top shelves of your closet and the floor under your bed as storage space, and keep the rest for everyday use. When you reorganize your closet, give the prime space to the clothes you wear most often. If you need more room in the closet, divide your clothes by season and find other storage options for off-season clothing. Make sure you have an effective system for doing laundry that includes time to properly put away clothing and iron, if needed. Another key to successfully reorganizing the master bedroom is making sure you've gotten rid of enough items.

This entire master bedroom is every-day space, so only keep things that you use regularly and enjoy in this space.

Closets seem to be the most difficult area, for women in particular. Here are some solutions to common problems people have with getting rid of items in their closets.

You're keeping it because you "spent good money" for it. If you're not wearing it often, then are you really getting your money's worth? I'm not talking about evening or holiday wear, but regular daily items. Do you have a friend who could get *your* money's worth out of the item? It would be great to see it on her, so you'd get value from giving away something precious and seeing it in use. Or go the opposite way—if it fits and you want to wear it more often, what could you buy to go with it so you'd increase the chances you'd wear the item? Do you feel it's worth the money to make another clothing investment?

It's hard to give up on the last chapter and move on. To that I say: Who are you today? What lifestyle do you live? Compare your lifestyle to how you want it to look. What's the gap, and why is there a gap? Have you moved on to a new chapter of your life and are just realizing the difference in clothing you need? Maybe you don't want to entirely give up on the last chapter of your life yet? You don't need to. Organizing and simplifying is not about getting rid of everything. It's about reducing, not eliminating. So keep some of your favorites from your last chapter. As you go through them, you'll figure out which are the favorites you want to bring forward into your new chapter. One client had spent her young married years living in another country that had a much different style of dress.

Several of her children were born in that country, and she forged lifelong friendships there. She had kept all her clothing from that era as mementos. We were able to reduce her collection, but we did not get rid of it.

Set boundaries. Decide on a fixed number for each type of clothing item. Having your own number is like giving yourself permission to let go. Write this number down and post it in your closet. If you find yourself with more than this number, you have too many and you need to cull. Use a one-in, one-out method. One woman chose twelve for the number of shoes she could have for each season. Another decided her growing children needed just three pairs of jeans, not the ten they each had. It was worth it to her, and the kids were of an age that it really didn't matter. They outgrew the clothes before they wore out. Another client used drawer space as a physical boundary. She'd allow one drawer for work-around-the-house clothing, two for lingerie, one for T-shirts, and so forth.

Keep a "donate" bag on your closet floor. When you try on something in the future and don't like it as much anymore, drop it into the bag. It's an easy way to keep up with culling out our old favorites. Normally, we put them right back on the closet rod, and then we revisit our decision many times! This is also a great way to make room for new clothes if you use the one-in, one-out method.

Designate a "probation" area for clothes you're not sure about. This can be a different part of your closet, or hang these clothes on a different type of hanger. Give yourself a deadline, and if you don't wear these clothes before the deadline, let them go.

Kitchen

Kitchens are difficult because they are the hub of the home. Kitchens are easily filled with clutter, and space is at a premium in this room. All of it is everyday space. Whenever possible, move nonessential kitchen items to your dining room, pantry, closet, or storage area. Bulk purchases, holiday items, supplies, and summertime utensils are examples of nonessential items.

So many activities take place in this room that it is essential that you clearly identify the functions of the room. Here are the typical functions of the kitchen and considerations for each function.

To eat in: How many people eat at home, and how often do you eat in restaurants? Do you still need enough everyday dishware to serve a large family, or can you keep just a few sets for everyday use? If you are an empty nester, you can keep a smaller amount of everyday dishes, glasses, and cooking items, while still keeping enough of your "nice dishes" for when your children visit. If you travel frequently or rarely eat at home, you don't need to hold on to as many dishes or cooking implements. What you don't need for everyday use can be stored elsewhere and out of your way.

Kitchens are easily filled with clutter, and space is at a premium in this room. All of it is everyday space. Whenever possible, move nonessential kitchen items to your dining room, pantry, closet, or storage area.

Hospitality: Do you host holiday dinners, and do you plan to continue this? Or is now a good time to pass along the legacy and the dishware? When my mother and father were downsizing, I offered to take over Thanksgiving dinner, and they agreed. So when they arrived for dinner, they brought the favorite family platters we'd used at their house and the Pilgrims history book we all read as children (back at least one generation), as well as Mom's favorite centerpiece. From my perspective, it felt almost like a ceremony, to take on the holiday but with all the fixings!

If you no longer plan to use your china and good silverware, could you find someone special in your family to gift it to? You can also sell to Replacements, Ltd., or companies like it, but be sure to have it appraised locally before you sell it if you have an older set. Sometimes the history of the piece makes it valuable, even if the pattern or maker's marks don't.

A place to sort mail and paperwork. My experience says many people sort their mail and handle household papers in the kitchen. Does this system work for you, or do your papers need a permanent home? The ideal solution is to have a household desk dedicated to the running of the household. Keep everything in one place. Another option is to process the mail in the kitchen and then move papers to wherever you'll need them: bills to the bill-paying box at your computer, homework to the kids' desks, medical papers to the household files, etc. Do you have a regular weekly time to clear the paper and deal with it? For my clients, I always try to find part of a shelf, kitchen cabinet, desk space, or section of countertop on which to sort the mail. Keep a container specifically for these papers in this area and clear it out regularly. You can clear it once a week or whenever the container gets full—whatever method works for you.

Kitchens have so many drawers and cabinets that it can be overwhelming to reorganize them. Here are some tips for how to handle each section.

Countertops. Countertops are clutter magnets! They are also prime everyday space. The key to keeping them clear is to have a defined purpose for your countertop. If an item doesn't serve that purpose, it doesn't belong on the countertop. The obvious purpose would be food preparation. If this is the case, you'll want a clear space with cooking tools nearby, perhaps contained in a jar or basket on the counter. You also may sort mail here. Have a container for the mail, whether it is a folder, a bin, or an accordion file. If you keep food on your counter, keep it in containers—a bread box, a basket or jar for snacks, a bowl for fruit. These containers keep like items together, make the most of the space, and limit how much you keep out.

Don't place something on the countertop because you don't know where else to put it. Clear space for it elsewhere, in a drawer, on a shelf, or in a cupboard. Take a few minutes at the end of the day to deal with loose items.

Cabinets. Cabinets are also clutter magnets because the doors let us easily hide our messes. As you rearrange the items in your cabinets, remember to keep like things together. Each cabinet should have a theme, and each shelf within the cabinet should contain no more than two or three groups of like items. If you have multiple groups on the same shelf, use containers or dividers to keep groups separated and organized.

Also remember everyday space. Place things where they are convenient to use—dishware near the dishwasher so it is easy to put away clean dishes and pots and pans near the stove where you use them. Keep seasonal items and rarely used items on high and low shelves. Keep regularly used items in easy-to-reach areas. This can save you fifteen minutes daily, just in the kitchen. If your mobility is limited, cull your items until you are able to keep everything you need within your range of motion. This may mean you keep only part of your dishware on a low shelf and put the rest on a higher shelf that can be accessed when guests visit.

Remember our phrase "someday is today." You can completely reinvent your dining room space.

Dining Room

How often do you use your dining room as a dining space, not a craft space, homework center, or drop zone for things that don't yet have a home in your house? Why not reorganize it into a room you can use every day instead of using it as a drop zone or saving the space for the few times a year you use it. Remember our phrase "someday is today." You can completely reinvent this space. Here are some practical ideas for how to use this space.

- A spacious study area. Whether you have children in school or are going back to school yourself, this is a practical function. It also keep papers out of your kitchen.
- A craft area. One client had many hobbies, including spinning yarn. She didn't have an extra bedroom for these hobbies, so we reorganized and reoutfitted the dining room as her hobby space.

- A music room. I helped a couple make this transformation. During most of their earlier married life, the musical instruments had been kept anywhere they could find space. The restructuring allowed them to keep all of their instruments and music in one place so they could enjoy them any time.
- A home-based work office. If you are starting your own business, you'll need a work space, and you may find, as one of my clients did, that the dining room is the only area available. If you use this area as an office, make sure all of your paperwork and office materials can be easily rolled away or hidden before company arrives.

Home Office

As you invent your new chapter, you may need a new or updated home office space. This is a permanent work space, different from your kitchen paperwork area or dining room study.

Here are some areas to consider setting up in your home office.

- Everyday workspace: desk, computer, technology, frequently used supplies in an easy-to-reach place, and the active files, separated by household and business.
- The creative space: open space and an open surface area where you can focus on just one project at a time.
- Near-term storage: for current and archived files, desk and PC supplies, music and software, books, or hobby supplies. Keep this close to your work space.
- Reference/archival storage: papers you know you need to keep, but you may not have to refer to them more than once a year.

"'Verb' your papers. Verbs are action-oriented, and when used on files and papers they suggest what to do with your papers rather than what they are called."

–JUDITH KOLBERG AND KATHLEEN NADEAU

Filing systems. The home office is home to your filing cabinet, too. These filing principles can be applied to both your own business and your personal files. If you run your own business, be sure to keep those files separate from your personal files so they are easy to access. If you're not used to filing, don't worry about a fancy filing system. The easiest way to remember where you've put a piece of paper is to figure out your instinctive reaction when asked, "Where or why would you look for this again?"

A client asked me the right place to file her insurance and auto repair papers. These are useful for business tax forms, but they are also personal expenses, and she thinks of them as "personal" papers. Do they get filed into an "all insurance" folder with car, home, and business insurance papers? Or with other home or car papers? Or with business expenses? The question I asked her was, "Where would you look for this paper the next time you need it?" Ask yourself that question for each paper and go with your gut. Don't make it more complicated than it needs to be.

"Work on one profit center at a time. Give a single project your full attention by keeping papers or items related to other projects out of sight. When it's time to move on to the next project, stash things related to the last project in a file or closet or drawer."

—BARBARA J. WINTER

Decide on your file categories. Use pencil to mark the folders, and just start to conquer those piles. If you want to have some fun, go out and buy a small label maker. Use file names that make sense to you. You also can use different colored or even patterned (think paisley, stripes, flowers, or polka dots) folders, which can cut down on the time you spend looking for a file because you can identify it by color in addition to the label.

Keep only files you use on a daily basis on or near your desktop. To hold these active files, you can use a wall file, clipboards that hang on hooks on the wall, a cascading desk stand, or simply pile them on the desktop. If you have a lot to reference, you can place them in a bin on the floor next to your desk, as one of my clients did. When she prepared taxes for a client, she had their bin by her side with the past year's tax files.

Another client working out of her home likes to work in two different rooms of the house. So she uses an accordion file to hold multiple files. The accordion file is easy to move around and keeps files together so they aren't spread around the house. Sometimes she needs an environment change to get motivated, so this is a great solution for her.

Bathrooms

Most homes have more than one bathroom. Why do you use one bathroom instead of the other? What needs to be in each space? It is perfectly fine to have duplicates of certain items, but you don't need to have a separate set of all your toiletries for each bathroom. Set limits for how many of each product you can have open at a time. Also try establishing a rule that you must finish a product or dispose of it (if you don't like it) before you open a new container of the same type of product.

> Set limits for how many of each product you can have open at a time. Also try establishing a rule that you must finish a product or dispose of it before you open a new container of the same type of product.

You also may use a bathroom for something other than grooming. Perhaps the downstairs bathroom also serves as the main area to change into swimsuits if you live on a lake or have a pool. Or you use the space to dry out winter wear. Or it could provide faster access for a medical need. Be sure to identify all of the functions for each bathroom and incorporate everything you need to support these functions.

If you've developed a medical or health challenge, how much space will you need for medicines and other paraphernalia? And where will these be used? Sometimes the bathroom is not the most useful place. It's more helpful to store these items where they are used, particularly if there are mobility issues. Medicines might be appropriate in the kitchen, if taken at mealtimes, for example. Some medications cannot be stored in the bathroom because of the humidity.

Break up the linen closet into zones: linens, toilet paper and other supplies, medical items, shower products, hair products, shaving products, less-often used products. A shelf or group of shelves can be a zone. You can also divide a single shelf into zones. Storage containers will help keep the zones intact. Be realistic about the amount of towels and linens you need for the number of people now living in your home.

Living Spaces: Living Room and Den

If you are welcoming a new energy into your home, whether it's a baby, a grandchild who visits often, or a puppy, be sure to childproof these areas as you reorganize. Put fragile items and potential choking hazards up high. You may want to make the room less formal as well, and introduce stain-resistant fabrics and flooring. Rearrange furniture to accommodate toys.

You also may want to arrange the room so you can store and use medical equipment and other paraphernalia here. Keeping the equipment in the center of the household keeps you from being isolated from other family members while you use it. The room also is comfortable and offers distractions if you need it. Home dialysis is a good example of something you may want to set up in a living area.

Here are some ideas and advice to use as you reorganize your living or den space.

Make the most of armoires, desks, and hutches. Evaluate what you have and arrange these pieces so you can make full use of their storage space. If you have too many pieces, consider getting rid of one or two. These can be clutter magnets. People often forget to organize inside these large furniture items. Keeping containers inside them forces you to find homes for everything you place inside. It also helps you make the most of space by letting you stack boxes on shelves. When buying containers, remember to measure first, order second.

Music and movies. Do you honestly listen to all the styles of music you own, or are some from another chapter of your life? Do you listen to CDs, or have you moved your music onto a new technology such as MP3s? If so, could you give away the CDs? You can do the same with movies you no longer watch. There are many donation options for music and movies you no longer love, from libraries to nursing homes to soldiers. We are a multigenerational community, so there will always be people who would enjoy your music, even on what you would consider older technology.

> When you let go of everything else, you'll make a lot more room in your storage area, which will make it easier to access and find the items you keep in storage.

Photos. The key with photos is first deciding on your favorites and then actually doing something with them, whether it's framing, scanning, or putting them in an album. How would you best enjoy them? Then you might realize you may not *want* to do as much with the others. It might be enough to put these other photos in a box.

Garage, Shed, Basement, and Attic

To successfully reorganize your storage areas, you must be sure you are keeping only the items you love and use. When you let go of everything else, you'll make a lot more room in your storage area, which will make it easier to access and find the items you keep in storage. If you have both a garage and a shed or both an attic and a basement, identify which items are best stored in each area. Consider temperature ranges, humidity, potential water damage, and where things are used as you make your decisions. In your mind, what is the difference between your attic and basement? Decide first on the primary types of items that will be stored in each space.

These storage areas are wide-open spaces, and there are a few ways to organize them:

- Divide up the space, either in your head or by taping off sections, to keep yourself within some boundaries. Use structures such as a closet, niche, or corner as a boundary. This is useful when it feels like you'll never get started because the space is so large. It's like using binoculars or a camera or blinders on an animal. Focus only on the area marked off in front of you; don't look at anything else.

- Make distinct sections (like departments in a store) for types of goods: car maintenance, workbench, gardening, and so on.

- Arrange boxes and bins in an orderly way. Place them on shelves or pallets to keep them off the floor for further protection and easier access. In the basement, use plastic bins, just in case of moisture.

- Move furniture to the perimeter of the room. Who you are storing the furniture for? Do they still want it? Have antiques appraised to help you decide whether to keep or sell them. If you kept the furniture thinking you would repair or refinish it someday, someday is now. Consider when or if this will really happen. Or give yourself a short-term deadline. If you're not sure what you'll do with the piece, think about giving it away or selling it. Or find out the cost to have someone else stain it or repair it for you so you can use the piece now.

- If you are still storing items for family, give them a deadline to take them away or you'll have them taken away. They have very likely forgotten what you have!

This wraps up our sections on reorganizing your home to support your life transitions. Next we move on to reorganizing your time.

PART THREE

Manage Your Time

TIME IS A PRECIOUS ASSET. Just as it's important for your home to stay in sync with who you are, it's important for your time and schedule to stay in sync with your values and priorities.

When you're going through a transition, your schedule is often turned on its head. Chapter eight is full of strategies to help you stay on top of all your commitments, both personal and professional, while making time for self-care during a time of transition.

Chapter nine will help you create a new framework to manage your schedule and time after your transition is complete and your time is your own again. Whether your transition has left you with more responsibilities and less personal time or has blessed you with more open, unstructured time, you'll find ways to effectively manage your schedule so you can keep your commitments, honor your priorities, and reach your goals.

8. Organize Your Time During Your Transition

UP TO THIS POINT, we've been discussing how to physically reorganize your house to fit your next life stage. In the following sections, we'll discuss solutions to different challenges you are going to have with your time and schedule as you begin, or continue, this transition toward your new chapter in your life. When we are preparing for a major life event, or we are in the midst of it, we know we have to organize our time to accommodate the change. We also need to organize our time for our own self-care because the emotional and physical drain is huge.

Organization, in times of crisis, can be a lifesaver. You can't organize your way out of everything, but you don't have to be a victim of circumstances either. You can organize so that you *feel* more in control. This life event is very likely an emotional one; you can't control the emotion or the pace at which you process it all, but you can adapt your behavior and manage your schedule to some degree. It's not an all-or-nothing approach, but doing something will help you feel like you're doing a lot.

MAKING THE MOST OF YOUR TIME DURING THE TRANSITION

There is a fair amount you can do both practically and emotionally as you move through this life event, but there also will always be situations, issues, and reactions no one can predict. Before you get into the details of setting your new schedule, look at the big picture and get a full idea of what you're dealing with so you are as prepared as possible. Here is some emotional and practical advice that can help you be as in control of your time as possible, realizing some events will be unpredictable. Out of order comes freedom.

Look for Deadlines

Some life events have a defined date, for example surgery or a divorce. This hard-and-fast date is actually helpful because it gives you a marker, a deadline, and an awareness that your change or event is indeed moving forward. So often, time seems to stand still when we have a major event happening.

You can't organize your way out of everything, but you don't have to be a victim of circumstances either. You can organize so that you feel more in control.

One summer, my housemate had to have a total knee replacement, the first of two. The surgery date, quite naturally, became a milestone, or what I call a manufactured deadline. Suddenly, the surgery date prompted all kinds of household projects that had to get done before surgery. We'd been talking for a while about some of these projects, and we certainly could have done the projects after surgery. But we used the surgery date as a deadline, and we got a lot done. The real benefit of these projects was that time moved along. We barely thought about the surgery during the month leading up to it, and that was a good thing in my household! Plus it made the time after the surgery less stressful because we could enjoy all of the improvements we'd made.

Other events that could spur you into action include finalizing your divorce, making room for an adult child or your parent to move in with you, or hosting out-of-town friends during a visit.

Other events have no defined date. For example, you're taking care of a parent, and you don't know what the future holds yet. In situations like these, you'll want to manufacture deadlines to help yourself feel like time is moving forward.

When you set a deadline, you get more done because you've made a commitment to finish the project or reach the goal by a certain time. Instead of thinking, *I'll get to it someday*, you can think, *I'll get it done before this day* and work to get it done. It's a very useful means to stay motivated or to give yourself a distraction or to put a marker in your life to know that time is passing. You will get through this event. Set deadlines, even if they are completely unrelated to the task at hand, to help keep you motivated and moving forward.

Get Advice From Friends who Have Been There

Talk to friends who have been through your same life event. What advice would they give? How did the event affect their schedules? What kind of time demands did they face? Consider their advice and experiences as you organize your calendar, appointments, and your master to-do list. Or seek out experts who can help you realistically assess your situation. You know in your heart that this life event is going to be emotionally tough, so rely on friends and experts, but understand that everyone is different. Don't worry if your journey is longer or shorter than your friend's.

For people going through a divorce, for example, you're going to need time with your attorney, your accountant, and for family mediation meetings. You'll need time to prepare yourself and your paperwork for these meetings. Ask your advisors how often they recommend meeting and balance this recommendation with your own perspectives. Or schedule a regular time each week to check in by phone. Even if you need other meetings, you'll have some of the time battle under control, and you'll each be accountable to the other for moving the process along.

SCHEDULE EVERYTHING

Determining deadlines helped you set a time frame for this transition (even if there is no official end date in site, as is the case with caregiving or empty-nesting). Consulting others who've been through similar situations helped you understand the time demands of this transition. Now you can begin fitting your new needs into your schedule.

As you begin your new chapter in life, there will be many new things to remember. Your old routines didn't include your new responsibilities, and you might not have formed new habits yet. You may find yourself forgetting things or missing appointments and that you're stressed and more distracted than usual. This is why you will find a written schedule so valuable in the midst of change. I suggest you use a portable day planner or calendar so you can keep it with you at all times. It can be paper or electronic, whatever you are comfortable with, but whatever style you choose, use only one calendar. When you have two or more calendars, you risk overlooking an appointment and missing information because it was recorded in one place but not the other.

> To make the best use of your time, have a plan for how you will use your time.

To make the best use of your time, have a plan for how you will use your time. Include regular commitments, responsibilities related to your transition, and be sure to fit in some time for fun, relaxation, and taking care of yourself, even if you have to schedule it. Planning your time takes some forethought. Start by identifying all of your commitments.

Mandatory Commitments

Start with schedules you must adhere to such as work or volunteer projects you already have committed to.

Family and household commitments. Now add the other household obligations that take up your time. Estimate the average amount of time these tasks require during a regular week as best you can. Examples of family and household responsibilities include:

- Appointments: drop-off, pick-up, doctors
- Fun/together time
- Household projects and repairs
- Meal planning/preparation
- Grocery shopping
- Bills/mail/paperwork
- Cleaning

These are tasks we know we have to get done, but often don't acknowledge how much time they take during the week. Without acknowledging that running a household takes a set amount of time, you'll end up rushing through, or not doing, some household tasks. Or you'll get them done, but the house or your time will be in disarray because you have "no time."

BALANCING YOUR NEW RESPONSIBILITIES WITH YOUR OLD

Now that you've laid out all of your obligations, you may be overwhelmed. How can you possibly accomplish all of this? The truth is, you can't and you won't. Unrealistic expectations cause unrealistic schedules. The reality is you are adding another job or role to your life, even if temporarily. I bet you weren't complaining beforehand that you had way too much time on your hands, were you? Your schedule was already full. So to add something to it, you'll first need to subtract something from it. It's natural to think that hobbies and interests are the first things that must go from a full schedule, but all work and no play isn't healthy. You need an outlet for your stress, and you need to preserve your individual identity, especially if you are in the role of a new parent or caregiver.

When it comes to children, pets, and household chores, you can't simply get rid of these roles in your life. Instead, you'll need to diminish the specific responsibilities of your roles. Now will be the time to put aside your pride, ego, guilt—or whatever motivates you—and respond "yes" when people ask if you need something or if they can do something for you. Asking for help is very difficult for some people. Maybe you're not used to relying on others. If so, think of it this way: Take the support they offer now, and make a promise to pay back the person when he is in a time of need. You can make the promise to the person or keep it as your internal promise so that you accept their assistance now.

So ask for what you need. Make it easier on yourself and others by being specific. If you live with others, what tasks can they take from you? Can someone else take over the responsibility of cooking? Or could you cook only one day a week, making large batches that can be frozen and reheated as needed on nights when you don't have time to cook? Can a family member move in for a couple of weeks to support you? Now is the time for creative thinking.

If you just can't bring yourself to rely on others, hire someone to help, when possible. At my house, for example, we had trash pickup for a few months immediately following the surgery and during the physical therapy that followed. Pay someone to mow your grass—a lawn care company or a teenage neighbor. Hire a pet walking service or a cleaning service.

BALANCE YOUR WORK NEEDS WITH YOUR PERSONAL NEEDS

Whether you are self-employed or work for someone else, you need to consider how your work will get done to your normal standards as you work through your transition. You could probably push through, still working your regular number of hours, but will you be focused enough to do work you'll be proud of? Probably not, due to all the emotion involved in your transition. And how much energy

Unrealistic expectations cause unrealistic schedules. Your schedule was already full. So to add something to it, you'll first need to subtract something from it.

Let go of items that, yes, ideally, could be completed before you change your work schedule. But just because you *want* to do these projects doesn't mean they *must* be done by you.

will you have for yourself and others involved in your transitional event?

Your task is to balance the two needs and come up with both a backup plan and a reasonable set of expectations for when you can partially and fully return to work. This is true even if you work for yourself.

As soon as you know a life event is coming up (maternity leave, for example), start thinking about each client and each project you work on and how you can prepare your colleagues, employees, or independent contractors for your departure or for fewer work hours and downgraded accessibility. The trick is to think creatively. If you're not particularly creative, find a friend or colleague and discuss it. Take a hard look at the details of each work responsibility you have. What current project could be wrapped up prior to your leave or shortening your workweek? What could potentially wait until afterward? What will be mid-project while you are out? Use this to create a master to-do list and to help you let go of items that, yes, ideally, could be completed before you change your work schedule. But just because you *want* to do these projects doesn't mean they *must* be done by you.

Consider the skills required for the client or project, and then review the skills of people you work with. If you're a solo entrepreneur, consider a trusted administrative person or assistant who could keep things together for the early days of your leave. Perhaps you've done this in the past when you took a vacation. If you still have time, try out someone to work with before you change your schedule.

Once you know who will do what, write down all of your instructions for each task. You'll need to communicate this plan more than once, so record it to make it easier on yourself. If you work for someone else, set up a formal meeting (even if it's over the phone) to review your backup plans and any issues you're concerned about, and then brainstorm together.

Change voicemail, e-mail auto-reply, and the like about two weeks before you'll be out or before you change your working hours as another reminder. As you get closer to the date, you can update these replies to direct people to your backups.

At home, for yourself and for those you live with, keep a list of who's doing what for you. Keep the list in one place and visible.

If You Must Work During This Transition Period

Try working half days. Set a low expectation. Bring your computer, or at least your to-do list (for both home and work), with you to work on when you are out and about managing your transition, such as going to appointments (doctor's or legal). You may not get to do anything, but sometimes you will have some waiting time, so be prepared. You'll relish the found time.

One of my clients drove a parent to the nearest city (which was an hour away) for medical treatments several days each week. She cut back on work hours, but also brought work with her. Sometimes she and her parent could spend time together during treatments, but sometimes her parent didn't want her around during the treatment, or her parent preferred to listen to music or watch a movie. So my client would bring a bag of things to do—some fun things, but also calls to make, medication lists to update, homework assignments to review, and so forth.

Another client, who was a business owner, cut back on her daytime business hours a bit, but she also began working an hour or two each night. She took on no new projects for a period of time.

Another business owner hired a virtual assistant, just for this difficult period, because she saw this as her best solution. Other people have hired errand services. It depends on what you're comfortable with and the kinds of tasks you'd be comfortable outsourcing.

Another business owner went into maintenance mode with her clients during her divorce. She knew if she added one more project to her work schedule, she would become overwhelmed and collapse. So she started an "after the divorce" list to record all of the projects she would tackle as soon as she felt able to focus more on work. Whenever a new idea would come to her, she would add it to the list so it could be addressed in the future without overwhelming her in the present.

Whether you're going through a divorce, going back to school after decades out, or caring for a parent, give yourself the time and the emotional space to do a job you'll be comfortable with and proud of. You won't regret it.

DETERMINING WHAT'S IMPORTANT

You've evaluated your time demands, opened your schedule to meet these demands by delegating household responsibilities, and restructured your work life. You now have a functional schedule to move forward with. How do you maintain your schedule as you work through day-to-day life? One of the easiest ways to maintain your schedule is to determine what is the most important use of your time and then devote your time to accomplishing those things first. If there's time left over, you've at least achieved the priorities.

> One of the easiest ways to maintain your schedule is to determine what is the most important use of your time and then devote your time to accomplish those things first.

When she first called me, Lisa had tried organizing her home on her own, but the stuff kept returning and she couldn't figure out why. She was in the middle of some major transitions. Lisa was about to turn fifty. Her daughter was a young teenager and becoming more self-sufficient. Lisa's mom had been diagnosed with Alzheimer's several years prior, but recently had suffered a significant decline, which required a new housing and living arrangement. When Lisa called, I asked her, "What matters right now?" In other words, what were the most important tasks she needed to deal with and keep organized? Her answers were:

- A system to handle her mother's medical, financial, and personal papers. This was a new responsibility that had been prompted by a change in Mom's living arrangements.
- A system to handle Lisa's family's papers and mail, especially as school started.
- A plan of attack, with room-by-room priorities, for organizing systems. She was overwhelmed with where to start. She didn't want a makeover, but wanted lasting systems.

Lisa was focused on reorganizing during her transition. Because these were priorities, she needed to carve out time in her schedule to work on each activity. Understand that you won't be able to reorganize everything during your transition. Pick the areas that need the most help and are the most relevant to your current situation. Notice Lisa wasn't worried about clearing her attic or reorganizing her craft supplies. She wanted to work on the systems that she needed to support her during her transition. Identify the systems you rely on and make it a priority to keep them in order. Systems make you more efficient, and because you're more productive, you gain time.

What Matters Three Months From Now?

When I asked Lisa what was important to her now, I also asked her what her values and her long-term goals were for her life. Her values were freedom, spirituality, and self-worth. Her ultimate goals: bring creativity, music, and/or writing back into her life; take care of her health so she'd be there for the significant events in her young daughter's life; be a better role model of life skills for her daughter; and figure out her own next chapter as her daughter continued to become more self-sufficient. I had her identify these values and goals so she could keep them in her mind and honor herself as she cared for her mother and daughter and also dealt with this transition. She needed this to set priorities on her time. She also needed this for her sense of purpose and self-identity amidst all the changes.

Identify your own values and goals. What is most important to you? What are your goals for your life? There are no wrong answers. And don't limit yourself by thinking a dream is impossible or you've waited too long to make it happen. If you want it, you can devise a plan to make it happen. If you don't dream, it can never happen for you.

After you've identified your values and goals, use them as guides so that as your schedule opens up, you can take small steps to reach these goals.

DANCE IN THE MOMENT

Dancing in the moment is a coaching skill. It means you relish the moment, letting it take you where it will. No agenda. No pressure. Let it be. And just be yourself.

The more organized, structured, or controlling you are, the harder it's going to be for you to take this all in stride and not go crazy from the stress. I see burn-out frequently. If you are a highly structured person, you can try a number of things to help you live in the moment.

- Look for someone who takes life in stride and model his or her behavior. Ask for advice on specific situations.
- Make a weekly date with a friend and talk about what's going on so you can verbally process everything.
- Consider seeing a life coach or therapist. A therapist can collaborate on the issues of your past that affect your behavior, attitudes, and self-esteem. A life coach looks forward with you, not into your past in any depth.
- Take up journaling. Much of the battle is acknowledging your true feelings and identifying the true cause of those feelings. Once you

delve a bit deeper into the real cause, you'll calm down. The issue is the confusion and vagueness around the emotions.

Decide how you will best process your emotions ahead of time so you get into the habit of taking care of yourself. What I mean is: When the situation is too much for you, how will you relieve stress? These life changes go on for a while. The change happens, but it's the transition into the next chapter that is exciting and frustrating at the same time. There's not much you can do to speed it up, and in that sense, it is similar to the grieving process. And you may in fact be doing some grieving, too, for another person, for a part of yourself, or for a chapter of life you've loved and are moving beyond now but will miss.

Preserve "Alone" Time

You may feel as if you need to continually focus on the transition to get through it. Don't lose yourself in this time. Take time to relax, to just be, to figure out the root causes of your emotions. Meditate, walk, punch a punching bag, read, pray, or listen to music—do whatever you usually do to keep your calm.

Have other people help you keep your daily commitment to yourself. Keep that "alone" time. It's useful for you, if not necessary for your health, and you'll be a stronger caregiver, parent, or whatever role you need to play.

TIME MANAGEMENT TROUBLESHOOTING

So you've mapped it all out and you're moving ahead creating your next chapter. And then real life sets in again, and it gets harder to keep to your plan. If you find yourself rushed, missing appointments, or running out of time, think about your time in relation to the Three Ps—people, products and process (see chapter three). What's your diagnosis of the issue with your time? An accurate diagnosis is key to figuring out which solution to use. Here are some typical time management issues and solutions.

Always Consult Your Calendar First

Where do you keep track of your appointments? Are they all listed in one calendar? Do you have two calendars? Do you write things on slips of paper? Set a limit with yourself—only use one calendar and write *every* appointment in it. This may seem strict, but in the long run, it is far easier to manage one calendar that has *all* of your events in it.

If you find your calendar doesn't help you keep track of appointments, perhaps you are using the wrong type of calendar. Calendars come in a wide variety of formats, from daily to weekly to monthly to quarterly, all on one page. If you use a daily view, maybe you're losing the forest through the trees, so try a weekly view instead. If you want to use your calendar as your place to list all your to-do's, the other things that don't have an appointment time, choose a format that has a list capability or space at the top or bottom of the pages for notes. Or if you love the calendar except for the lack of a notes section, add a notepad into the calendar or clip paper to one of the covers so you have your list.

If you forget the calendar, and someone wants to book an appointment, call the person later, when you have your calendar in front of you and can stop to think about what day and time would be best.

Or maybe you're using technology for your calendar. If that's the case, be sure everyone in your family or household has a way to see the calendar, too. If you carry your calendar on a smartphone, sync it with the family computer so everyone can see the calendar. Or maybe everyone in the house uses the same technology; for example, everyone uses a smartphone device. Make sure the other members know how to sync their devices and that your settings are only one person's responsibility so there are no mix-ups. The easiest option I've found is to "invite" household members to appointments they need to know about or need to be part of. So in my case, all of my evening classes, business meetings, or personal appointments include my household members as invitees, but it's really just for their information. This way, if I forget to communicate about an evening I'm out, at least that appointment shows up on all calendars. It's a safeguard and a planning tool; it does not replace communication.

Carry your calendar with you all the time, even around the house. Put it alongside other items you always take with you when you leave your home (purse, wallet, keys, glasses, or cell phone). If you forget the calendar and someone wants to book an appointment, call the person later when you have your calendar in front of you and can stop to think about what day and time would be best. When we make fast decisions about appointment times, we set ourselves up to be rushed and overbooked.

Household Weekly Meetings

Make it a point once a week to review your upcoming week, whether you live on your own or with others. Saturday or Sunday is a good day to do this. The meeting means you will have more time for any necessary prep work such as making special purchases for the week, setting up a car pool, or scheduling an appointment. If you live with others, make sure everyone is around when you review the upcoming week. Also quickly check in each day in case something has changed. The best time to do this is at dinner or later in the evening. Have the calendar handy and ask everyone to go over their schedules for the next day. Even with calendars and written appointments, some people keep their schedule in their heads, so you still need to communicate changes.

Include Travel Time

Check to be sure you have "departure time" listed for all appointments. Often, we put the appointment start time on the calendar and forget that we have to allow ourselves time to get to the appointment. What time do you need to leave the house to make it to your appointment on time? Time yourself one day to see how long it typically takes you to get ready and leave the house. Then add that time and travel time to the calendar. It could look like this: Volunteer at library at 2:30, leave house by 1:50. If you will be traveling with young children, an elderly person, or a person with mobility issues, double the time you expect it to take to travel somewhere. Giving everyone plenty of time will reduce stress and rushing.

Build in Transition Time

Check whether you have enough transition or travel time in between places you need to be. Just as you write the travel time on your calendar, write an end time on your calendar. Even if you are cleaning the house in the morning before an appointment, set a time when you will finish so you have time to get yourself ready and head out the door on time. We all fall into the habit of thinking, *One more thing before I leave.* A favorite phrase I use for myself is, "Do one less thing," because I'm always tempted to squeeze in one more task.

Consistently Contain Items That Leave the House

Do you find yourself forgetting items you need to take with you when you leave the house? Do you consistently run back into the house after getting in the car because you've forgotten something? Establish a consistent place for the things you need to take with you each day as you leave. This can be, for example, a bench near your front door, a series of hooks behind the closet door or on the hallway wall, or the top shelf of the front hall closet. Get those items together the night before; most people find it easier to think about the details the night before and not in the morning when we have less time to get out the door and may not be fully awake. Once you have this place established, return items to it as soon as you enter your home so you don't need to hunt them down later. See my example on page 51 for an idea of how this works.

If you can't figure out where your time goes, keep track for a day. Record what you did each quarter hour or at least half hour. Sometimes we're doing much more than we knew. Or it can be that an activity or task took more time than we realized.

Schedule in Daily Household Chores

Do you find yourself squeezing in time for grocery shopping or cleaning, and it's always too rushed? Try selecting two days or evenings a week as "shopping time" or "cleaning time." I suggest two because most people's schedules are too variable to use the same day/time each week. But having an alternate works. Or, review your schedule every Sunday night and plot in when you'll shop or clean; make it an appointment you keep.

I hope this chapter answered your question of "How am I going to get through this?" with some time management techniques. Imagine if you were to let your time and your schedule run your life during this tough time. Wouldn't that be just one more stressor on top of an already-tough situation you're in? Gaining some control over your time will reduce your stress and will help you feel like you do have some control over your life at this time. Remember, you already had a busy life before this life-changing event occurred. You're piling on more responsibilities, when you already had a full plate, so try some of the ideas in this chapter. Make them your own so they work for you in your own situation.

9. After the Event: What Does Your New Schedule Look Like?

THE PREVIOUS CHAPTER HELPED YOU ORGANIZE YOUR SCHEDULE as you dealt with your life transition. This chapter will help you organize your time and schedule after the transition is complete and you have settled into a "new normal." Approach this chapter after you've had time to begin to accept your new circumstances in life. Now that the transition is complete, are you finding it difficult to adjust to your more open or more crowded schedule? Can you relate to any of these quotes?

> *I spent so much time taking care of my mom, and now she's gone. What will I do with my time now?*

> *We got through the surgery and things are finally back to normal, but life seems, well, a little boring. I have time I didn't have before.*

> *The divorce is final, at last, and the kids are pretty self-sufficient. I feel like I have all this free time to do what I want to do. I'm free to be me! But now what?*

> *The kids are out on their own, and we are officially empty nesters. So what's next?*

I'm retired and love it. I know how I would like to spend my time, but I can't seem to structure my day or be purposeful with my time.

Many people fear a blank slate, but if you look within yourself, you'll find that you have plenty of interests and ambitions to fill that slate. Some of you will want to revive past interests you let go of for various reasons. There is comfort in returning to something familiar as you explore and add new interests as well. Other people will leave behind anything old and want to start completely fresh and new. They are comfortable with a completely blank slate and enjoy the adventure of learning new things.

The answers to the "what's next" questions are inside you; you just haven't asked the questions in a long while. You've been caregiving or parenting or grieving, and that process was necessary and required much of your energy. Only you can figure out how you want to fill your time now; however, I'll give you key questions to reflect on to discover your answers. It's time to focus on you, again, which may feel odd or uncomfortable at first—like a muscle that's not been exercised in a while. Start slowly and build your interests over time.

One of the benefits of today's complex world is that we are much more open to change. As our lives have become more complex and split into smaller and smaller pieces, we've learned to handle change more easily. The old adage was to have a five-year plan. We were told to create a vision for our work life, our personal interests, or our entire life, a vision that could be achieved in five years. I've used the visioning process myself and always found the process, rather than the result, to be enlightening. Now I go through that process at least once a year. In today's world, five years is too far off on the horizon.

WHAT MATTERS NOW?

It can be overwhelming to try to plan the entirety of your next chapter in life at the very beginning of it, so don't get bogged down in making a five-year or even one-year plan yet. The key question to ask yourself is, "What matters, right now?" Use short-term thinking and identify *now* versus *not now*. The second question is, "What do I know about what I want?" The answers to both of these questions are already inside you. To illustrate this, let's revisit Lisa's story from chapter eight.

We discussed how Lisa was dealing with her teenage daughter's growing independence and her mother's declining health. Her story continues from there. Lisa's mother passed away about a year after I began working with Lisa. She had spent so much time caring for her mother, and now she would need to fill that time with something else. Time was a blank slate. After her mom died, I asked Lisa to identify "What matters now?" and "What matters three months from now?" I had asked her those same questions a year earlier. Her answers now were much different because she was in a different place.

What mattered now, in the immediate time frame, was:

- Time to grieve
- Going through some of her mother's things
- Spending time with family
- Getting away for the first time in a long time
- Getting back to normal routines for school and around the house

> It can be overwhelming to try to plan the entirety of your next chapter in life at the very beginning of it, so don't get bogged down in making a five-year or even one-year plan yet.

- Time to just "be" for a while, to let the grief happen, and to accept that the days no longer include visits with Mom

And what mattered three months from now:
- Do something new for her daughter, specifically renovating the bonus space to give her a new bedroom.
- Finish up the home-organizing coaching so the first round of decluttering is done. She had decided earlier to do rounds of organizing and coaching through the house. As she worked through each room, she sensed that her tolerance for "stuff" was declining. This often happens when someone you love passes away. Death is a reminder that we are not our stuff at all. Making two organizing rounds helps process the grief in time and in stages.
- Begin figuring out what "spirituality" means to her by exploring and reading.
- Think about what the holidays will be like. What new traditions would she like to start on her own? How would she honor her mother? How would she deal with the grief?

And that was it for her three-month plan. More would come later as she figured out her next chapter, but this was enough for her. As you consider your next step, divide your wishes into time segments and take small steps, instead of believing you can define and create your new chapter right away. Let it unfold. Life events and change take up a lot more of your energy than you realize.

MEETING YOUR IMMEDIATE GOALS

After you identify what matters, you'll need to figure out how to achieve those goals and honor those priorities. As Lisa's example shows, they aren't always easy. After all, how do you specifically take time to grieve? Here are some ideas that will help you identify action steps you can take to meet your goals.

Hire a life coach or Certified Organizer Coach®. Both are trained and certified in helping people work through self-exploration and issues such as determining the next steps in life. They are also trained in methods that will allow you to reinforce lasting change. They ask insightful, powerful questions to aid your thinking process. This is a helpful option particularly if you need to talk through ideas to process them or need an accountability partner to keep you focused and moving along in your process.

Read a book about the type of transition you're completing. For example, a book about life after divorce or a career-coaching book. These books have advice on what's next and are targeted to a specific issue. Books give you examples and advice. It's up to you, or you and your coach, to apply these ideas to your life and goals.

Read a more general book about creating your next chapter. I read *What's Next: Women Redefining Their Dreams in the Prime of Life* by Rena Pederson. She wrote case studies of women, famous and not, who had figured out a next chapter, so you read a variety of ways to figure it out. And she provides exercises to walk you through the process. A few clients have recommended *I Could Do Anything If I Only Knew What It Was* by Barbara Sher.

Attend a workshop. In my workshop, titled Give Your Life a Makeover: What's Your Next Chapter?, a life coach and I provide participants with our approach to getting through the overwhelming feelings they experience when thinking about their next chapter. We provide a framework to work through goals for the participants' next chapters.

Journal about it. Whether you write it down, use a tape recorder, or create a piece of art representing your feelings and ideas, the idea is to get the thoughts out of your head. Over time, any of these methods will get you to the deeper levels of thinking, which is where those answers are.

Spend time with a close friend and figure it out together. Start asking friends how they got through this period in between the last chapter and the new one.

Questions to Help You Take Action

These are the key questions to ask yourself as you decide what to do and how to spend your time in your next chapter. Some we have reviewed earlier, but now you are actually creating the next chapter, so let's get back to them. Take time to reflect on each of these questions.

- What do you value? What is important now?
- Where are you doing the best in your life? Or living the best version of you? What's working well?
- Which facet of your life would you like to improve?
- What do you currently know about what you want next?
- What do you know about your vision or about your ideas for your next chapter? Write it, paint it, say it aloud—whatever works to keep it alive.
- What is holding you back internally?
- What do you need to let go of? What makes it difficult to let go? What do you need or what questions can you ask yourself to make a no-regrets decision and move on?
- What is important to keep with you going forward? What is now permanently part of your being, your core, your essence?
- What has this life event taught you about yourself?
- How can that new information help you create your next chapter?
- How have you created something from nothing (or very little) in the past? What principles, ideas, or actions from that experience can you apply to this new experience?
- What are the major accomplishments in your life? How did you approach and achieve them?

- What is one goal you can limit yourself to for now? It's important to start and finish one goal and then move on to another. If you start several at once, it's difficult to sustain momentum because your first success takes longer. A success, no matter how small, feeds you.
- How will you know when you have achieved that one goal? How will you realize it, feel it, or see it? What does it look like or feel like when you've achieved the goal?
- What are the smallest steps you can take to begin chipping away at your goal?

FOCUS ON YOUR PRIORITIES

From your answers to the questions above, you'll have a list of goals and, therefore, priorities for your time. Goals become priorities only after you rank them in order of importance to yourself. Take time to sort out all your goals and figure out which has top priority. Each goal has priority in your life, but ranking them shows you where you want to start.

Goals become priorities only after you rank them in order of importance to yourself. Take time to sort out all your goals and figure out which has top priority.

Usually your number one priority will be income if that was affected by your transition. You'll want to be sure that your basic and practical needs are taken care of before you focus on the "want" side of life. After that, rank the goals in terms of your current satisfaction with each area of your life. Life coaches have specific exercises to work you through these. If you are working on your own, list all your goals. Rank them by your current satisfaction. Think of each goal's value to you, relative to the other. Or use a scale of 1–10, where each number can only be assigned to one goal. Or use the terms "very satisfied," "usually satisfied," or "hardly satisfied." Note if there are goals you are already working on, so even if that goal score is low, you know that you're already at work on that facet of your life.

Some people use the bucket list approach. This is the "Before I kick the bucket, I want to …" list. Some limit themselves to a number, perhaps two new activities per year or quarter. Last, if none of your goals sparks an immediate interest in you, then choose any goal and just get started.

If you find yourself with "too many" interests, read *Refuse to Choose!* by Barbara Sher. She writes that some people have many interests and it's okay. Traditionally these people are thought of as dilettantes or as a jack-of-all-trades but master of none. She writes that some people are quite capable of deeply knowing many hobbies and are so curious that they need many activities. So it's a positive to have "too many" interests. If this is you, keep your schedule manageable by choosing two new interests at a time and focus on those for a month, a quarter, a year, or for as long as you find them interesting. And then switch to other new interests. Keep a list or a journal of what you're interested in next so you don't lose good ideas.

For the first time in a while, perhaps, you'll have no one to tell you whether your answers are good, right, wrong, worthy of your time, or not.

GIVE YOURSELF PERMISSION

So for the first time in a while, perhaps, you'll have no one to tell you whether your answers are good, right, wrong, worthy of your time, or not. You decide. Get rid of those nagging thoughts that say, *What would Mom have wanted?* or *What would my husband have said?* To get rid of these thoughts, you'll need to replace them with new thoughts, and that will take practice. For example, practice thinking, *What do I want?*, Or *I get to decide. This is fun.* Or *What do I need?* And say the word *I* in a louder voice than the other words in the question, just for the positive reinforcement. Repetition works, and it doesn't take as long as you might think. Choose your phrase,

Schedule Chart

MONDAY	TUESDAY	WEDNESDAY	THURSDAY

your mantra, or your new outlook and practice it out loud. I have never been one to say affirmations out loud. I write them down and post them on a bulletin board I see every day. I believe we attract what we think. So if the out loud practice doesn't appeal to you, try to whisper the phrase under your breath so you hear what it sounds like. That also worked for me really well. Or at least take a moment to intentionally think that thought as you start your day.

I often hear this comment from pre-retirees and retirees: "I'm busier than I've ever been, even compared to raising my children!"

KEEPING STRUCTURE IN YOUR SCHEDULE

I often find that if someone's been tightly tied to a schedule, it's easy to throw away the entire schedule once she has some freedom. But a little bit of structure will allow you to focus on your new interests and do something with them. Some people need structure

FRIDAY	SATURDAY	SUNDAY

to prevent discouragement from setting in during tough times. Others find structure early in the day gives them something to wake up for. And sometimes that lack of structure translates into the thought that we have plenty of time to start a new interest and then we don't quite get around to it because there's no rush. That was definitely my issue when I was out of work. I had no structure, so I frittered away my days. That was okay for a while, to give myself time off. But after a while, I needed a purpose.

To make the best use of your time, create a plan for how you will use your time. Think about how you planned your time in chapter eight. The process is much the same, but instead of adding new obligations and responsibilities, you'll have time to add new interests and hobbies.

Mandatory Commitments
Start with schedules you must adhere to, such as work or volunteer days and hours. List those commitments in the chart on this page.

Family and Household Commitments

Now add the other household obligations that take up your time. Estimate the regular weekly time commitment as best you can. Again, it's important to acknowledge how much time it takes to run a household; otherwise you'll neglect some tasks and rush through others.

New Interests

Now you'll decide on which one or two new activities or interests you want to add. Or maybe it's one or two new friends you want to get in touch with again. Choose just one or two and absorb them into your schedule. If you then find you can handle more, add more. You don't want to tire yourself out after everything you've just been through. Build things gradually. You may find you enjoy a slower pace.

Here are some examples of activities you might add. Let it inspire you to brainstorm your own ideas. Go back to your values and see if you find some clues there.

> Think about some loose guidelines you can create so you don't end up with an overcrowded schedule that keeps you from enjoying the moment.

- Exercise
- Crafting
- Reading
- A hobby group or club: singing, writing, collecting, needle arts, sports, book club
- Musical instrument
- Weekly or monthly night out with friends
- A social group/place to meet new people
- Travel, local and long distance
- Events: concerts, festivals, museums, libraries. By joining some of these organizations or adding yourself to the newsletter list, you're reaching out to find new hobbies.
- Volunteering

What's your preference? Think about some loose guidelines you can create so you don't end up with an overcrowded schedule that keeps you from enjoying the moment. Decide on how much time you want to spend outside your home. For some people, this equates to how many evenings they want to be out per week. For others, they're out a lot on the weekends, but like staying in on weekday evenings. Or, if you're looking for less structure, let your schedule grow organically and see where your interests lead you. If you go the organic route, set a trial period for activities so you don't feel guilty about needing to drop an activity if you find your schedule is too full. Know your limits and don't be afraid to say no.

If you're on a budget you may feel as if you shouldn't spend any money on fun because necessities are more important. But you'll be more successful if you build in times to treat yourself. Give up coffee at the coffee shop just a few times one week, and you'll have a ticket to a local concert, museum, festival, or something else you might enjoy.

MAKE PROJECTS MANAGEABLE

Are you overwhelmed by large tasks on your calendar? Break up your projects, goals, and new interests into smaller, workable pieces so you make gradual progress. For example, if you want to take an art class, break it down into steps: first, research the classes available; second, select the class; third, register for the class; fourth, get the materials list for the class; fifth, purchase the materials; sixth, attend the first class; seventh, schedule time to work on your art projects outside of class.

"Put down everything you can imagine you might ever want to accomplish. Don't be limited by *anything*—time, money, geography, or past failures. Remember your childhood dreams and ask yourself if you would still like to try for some of them."

– DOROTHY LEHMKUHL & DOLORES COTTER LAMPING, *ORGANIZING FOR THE CREATIVE PERSON*

This is a difficult skill to learn because it requires you to see the big picture first and then break it down into details. Some people see only the big picture, and others see only details.

Here are some different approaches to breaking up life goals into workable pieces.

- *Use the phrase "one step closer."* Ask yourself what is one step you can take right now to bring you closer to your goal.
- *Index cards.* Keep track of all the steps using index cards. Write one step per card.
- *Sticky notes* are a useful tool to help your brain isolate one step at a time. Then move them around into the order to work through.
- *Folders.* If your goals have papers associated with them, make one folder for each goal so everything stays in one place. And keep the folders in one consistent place, too, so you can always find them. For home projects, treat yourself to some fun, beautiful file folders. For major projects like a home renovation, you can purchase "project" folders. On the outside of the folder, there is a preprinted form to list your steps and check them off as you get them done.

After you've separated your large goal into these smaller steps, it becomes easier to find time to work on your new hobby or go to school or look for that new career.

- *Tape recorders* are a great option for verbal or auditory people who find it easier to talk things through rather than write them out. Whether at your desk, at home, while taking a walk, or in the car, pick your topic and start talking out the steps. After you've recorded the steps, you can write them up on a list, on index cards, or use software that does it for you.
- *Drawing pictures or mind mapping* are fun and visual options. The concept behind mind mapping is that you're creating a map of

what's on your mind. By using pictures, shapes, icons, and words, if you like, you'll generate a diagram of those small, workable pieces that make up your goal. Starting in the middle of a piece of paper (flip chart size is particularly fun, but standard-sized paper works just fine), draw a picture of or write your project or goal or activity name. From the center, start writing whatever is in your head. Don't be concerned about ordering the steps. Just let your mind go. If you find you have lots of ideas related to one aspect, connect those ideas to each other. I think of this as brainstorming with yourself. When you've run out of ideas and thoughts about the topic, you can start ordering the pieces or transferring them in order to a sheet (or index cards, your planner, etc.) you can work from

After you've separated your large goal into these smaller steps, it becomes easier to find time to work on your new hobby or go to school or look for that new career. The goal feels smaller and more achievable because you're not taking on the entire goal at once. You're simply taking the next step toward the goal, and eventually all of those steps add up.

You're on the other side of this life event or series of life events. You've spent time reflecting on how to create your next chapter, how life could be different, and what possibilities you could take advantage of with more time to do so. Our next and last chapter will focus on organizing systems that help your household run smoothly, giving you more time for these new possibilities.

PART FOUR

Staying Organized

YOU'VE COMPLETED YOUR HOME MAKEOVER. Congratulations. That is integral to you moving on in your new chapter in life. Now, how do you maintain this level of organizing so you're not forced into another makeover in a few months?

The answer is to set up organizing systems that you can seamlessly incorporate into your everyday life. These systems will allow you to run an orderly, efficient household, spend the least amount of time possible on chores, and share responsibilities with other members of your household. Plus, systems make it easier to do a great job every time, whether it's paying bills on time or effectively handling household paperwork.

10. Create Systems That Support You

WITH ANY MAJOR CHANGE IN YOUR LIFE, chances are your organizing systems will need to change somewhat. This happens for a variety of reasons. I'll mention a few here.

- You may not have been the one who created the systems in your household. Now you are responsible for maintaining them, and the systems your household used to follow don't seem to work as well anymore. Or the systems don't play to your strengths.
- You've added people to your household. They—whether adults or children—need to adopt your systems, and they're not adopting them as easily as you thought they would. And sometimes systems have to be adjusted because they really were designed just for you; but now you're married or taking care of children, grandchildren, or a parent.
- You're merging households with a new spouse or partner. You've each lived with another and lived on your own for a while, so co-creating new systems will be important to your relationship and the new household.
- You've shifted from working at an office outside the home to running a business at your house or telecommuting.

- The organizing systems were designed for a family, and you're approaching, or are in, the empty-nest phase.
- Just as friendships and relationships are healthiest when we grow, change, and learn together, our organizing systems need to grow and change to work the best for us. This is particularly important to watch for as you move in and out of life's major events.

We hear the phrase "new normal" a lot these days, usually in a financial context. But this phrase can also be applied to your life after you've completed a major transition or started a new chapter. A client first used this phrase to describe her life after we had finished the first run-through of organizing her home. Due to several sequential life changes, she'd let her house become disorganized. As we worked together to reorganize, she talked about her "new normal" being that time in the future when her household and life were again organized the way she wanted.

As we reorganized her home, my client experienced a lot of emotions and shifts in her mind-set. She learned how to let go of objects *and* attitudes or beliefs she no longer needed or wanted. She understood better how to motivate herself to get started on an organizing project, how to stick with it, and how to finish it to 100 percent, not her usual 80 percent with things left undone at the final stages. She realized how to work with the other people in her household and understood what she could count on them for. She also set up realistic expectations for maintaining the organizing we'd collaborated on.

You've now made your home and your schedule begin to reflect the new you, the person you are becoming.

If you've been organizing as you've been reading this book, hopefully you've experienced these same shifts. You've now made your home and your schedule begin to reflect the new you, the person you are becoming. What other systems will you need to revisit or establish as you move out of the REORGANIZE phase and into the maintenance phase?

As you enter the maintenance phase, it's important you have a clear understanding of all of your duties and responsibilities. Think of yourself as the CEO of your household. Some surveys put the value of the household CEO at more than $100,000. It's a tough job with little training. You manage the activities of your household, whether it consists of multiple people or only you. You manage schedules, handle the finances, outsource to service providers when needed, delegate, and deal with discipline and rewards. You run the household as a small business. Effective organizational systems make parts of this CEO position much easier for you and for the household.

The organizational responsibilities of a household CEO fall into five categories:

1. Time management
2. Financial
3. Meal planning
4. Household chores and maintenance
5. Paperwork

This chapter will equip you to maintain the new organizing systems you've created and help you stay in control of your home and your schedule for the months and years to come. It will teach you how to establish organizing systems that will allow you to effectively carry out your duties in each household category. With simple and useful systems in place, you can efficiently handle your responsibilities so you have more free time to do things you enjoy. This, to me, is the main reason for staying organized.

Evaluate each of these systems whenever it feels as if you are losing control of them. Take extra time to figure out what has changed. It could be as simple as you've stopped following your schedule or routines.

Evaluate each of these systems whenever it feels as if you are losing control of them. Take extra time to figure out what has changed. It could be as simple as you've stopped following your schedule or routines.

When things are going well, it's easy to think you can be more flexible and let things slide, but it doesn't take long to realize that routines actually help make things easier. If you find you need more help or motivation, consider collaborating with a Certified Organizer Coach®.

TIME MANAGEMENT

Chapters eight and nine are full of time management ideas. The best way to stay in control of your time is to set routines for your busiest times of day. Those times tend to be the morning and evening. Think about the evening and the morning as one block of time, so evening runs right into morning. Do as much prep work as possible the night before so you can whittle down the morning routine to fairly standard pieces and eliminate as much last-minute rushed thinking as possible. In most households, it's harder and takes longer to get everyone going in the morning, yet we have less time in the mornings. Even if you are an early bird, others may not be.

> The best way to stay in control of your time is to set routines for your busiest times of day.

Managing Your Morning Routine

Set your morning routine by listing all the things you must do to prepare for the day ahead. When you finish the list, think about this question: Which things can be done the night before? Pack everything that's needed for the day the previous night. Lay out outfits. Pack lunches. Get directions. Put your pocketbook, cell phone, and keys in one spot—the same spot every day—as you come in the house so you don't need to search for them in the morning.

After moving as many items to the evening as possible, estimate how much time each remaining item will take you in the morning. Then list the things you would *like* to do and estimate how much time these items will take. Consider asking other household members to handle more, or at least their own, chores. Children as young as four and five years old can learn and work through some of their responsibilities. Older children, once they have a list of responsibilities, can do more on their own. Teach them and let them try.

Determine when you need to leave your house to be on time (include the time it takes to load and unload the car and walk from the parking lot, plus extra minutes for traffic delays). Then use this departure time to determine your wake-up time. Be sure you are giving yourself enough time to accomplish everything on your list.

Track Your Routine to Find Problems

If things aren't working out, track everything that happens each morning for a week. At the end of a week, review your notes to see if there are any patterns. Is one child always running late? Are you always late with your own stuff? Is breakfast taking too long? Are you behind because you're the only person keeping track of everyone? Are you getting out on time, but always leaving something behind? Usually we are either trying to jam too much into the morning, or we don't realize how long things take. A twenty-minute drive may become a forty-minute excursion when you add in the time it takes to load the car, drive, find a parking space, unload, and walk into the building to get settled.

Identify the problem and then find a solution. We often don't delve in and figure out where the problem specifically is. You might need to change a wake-up time, eliminate a morning activity by doing it the night before, delegate more, or create a checklist so you always leave with everything you need.

Account for Added or Extra Activities

Another reason things may go out of balance is that you've added something to your schedule without readjusting it. When we add things, we tend to mark only the actual event in our calendars. But we often don't make the time for all of the small, seemingly insignificant preparation tasks associated with the event, and that's where we end up rushing around and forgetting things.

For example, you may decide to start going to the gym three days a week, so you mark those days on your calendar. Now think about all the extra activities associated with going to the gym—gather and launder dirty gym clothes, pack clean clothes into the gym bag, figure out your schedule and whether you need to pack your work clothes, figure out lunch plans, and leave at a different time that day. We often try to add in this activity without realizing there are many preparation steps before we can get into the car to drive to the gym.

Another reason things may go out of balance is that you've added something to your schedule without readjusting it. When we add things, we tend to mark only the actual event in our calendars.

So when you add a new activity to your schedule, list all the things you need to do related to that activity and accommodate these new tasks into your existing routine. You can do it. You just need to plan for it.

Weekly Review

In addition to a morning and evening routine, a weekly review will help you manage your time. At the start of the week (Saturday or Sunday), take fifteen or twenty minutes to reflect on the week ahead. Pull out your calendar and make note of activities. Ask each member of your household if they know of any activities in the coming week that are not on the calendar and add them. Review (or create) your meal plan (plan easy meals for busy nights). Set your to-do list for the week to meet future deadlines or accomplish tasks. Have a plan for each day and move things around if you end up with too much on any day. Make sure car pools are set. Get cell phone numbers into your phone. Put errands on your calendar so you can do them when you know you'll be in that area. Looking ahead will help you prepare, and you'll avoid last-minute rushes and hectic days. And if you need to move an appointment, you can do it early and avoid cancellation fees.

FINANCIAL MATTERS: MONEY IS NOT THE ROOT OF ALL EVIL

As you enter this "new normal," you'll want to know the state of your financial affairs, where you've been, where things are headed, and what you need to do to plan ahead. The worst thing you can do is to bury your head in the sand and hope for the best. There are classes, articles, independent financial advisors, and experts who can set up these systems and do the tracking with you. Notice I say "with you" and not "for you." While a hired professional can advise you in any of these areas, it is your money and your future. Nobody will take as good care of it as you will. So follow your instincts. Learn about these areas, even if you hire someone to support and collaborate with you. Ask friends who've been through similar life events how they built financial knowledge.

Bills and Expenses

If you are paying your bills on time, keep with whatever system is in place for now. You've just been through a major life event, so if something is working, don't fiddle with it now. Keep something stable. I've always heard that after some significant event occurs, we are better off not making any major changes for a year. Emotionally, we are probably not quite ready for more change.

Begin to understand where the money goes by tracking your expenses. What are your biggest expenses? What expenses are flexible while still allowing you to maintain your present lifestyle? The simplest tracking method is to look back as you pay your bills this month. Then look at the last few months to get a sense of roughly how much each bill is over time.

Look at the data, but also add your judgment; you are the only one who will know why a certain expense was oddly high in a particular month and whether that's a trend or not.

Another tracking method is to download transactions from your online bank statement, or if you pay checks manually, start a log, journal, or spreadsheet. Track expenses for three typical months (that is, not over holiday months or vacation). Take an average of how much you spend. Use software or an expense-tracking or cash-flow tracking sheet. Check monthly and annual expenditures; is this how you want to spend your income, or has this developed as a habit over time?

If something is working, don't fiddle with it now. Keep something stable. I've always heard that after some significant event occurs, we are better off not making any major changes for a year.

And of course, if you use cash, keep track of all those small expenses, because they add up quickly. Keep a notebook or put the expenses into your PDA, even if it's sending yourself an e-mail.

Once you know you have your expenses down on paper, so to speak, actively manage your money. Subscribe to blogs about thrift or simplicity. Use Quicken, www.Mint.com, or a similar site to continue tracking and watching your money.

Tracking for Taxes

If preparing your taxes is an unfamiliar task that will be part of your "new normal," this is a great time to ask for outside expertise. You don't necessarily need to hire someone to handle your taxes for the rest of your life, but for now, following a major life event, it might be a good idea. Chances are high that this life event will affect the claims you can make on your taxes or the way you will file taxes. So talk to friends to get a referral and set up an informational meeting.

The year I had all my big life changes, a bank manager I trusted recommended a certified public accountant to prepare my taxes. At the time, I thought I'd just ask him to prepare the taxes for a year or two and then use those years as a model and do them myself. But I had divorced, moved states, and eventually set up my own business, which made my tax situation too complex for me to understand. So, more than ten years later, I'm still working with that tax professional. For me, the cost is worth it because it saves me stress and time. Could I figure out my taxes? Probably. Do I choose to spend my newfound time that way—no thanks. I gave up other things to pay for this service, and I gained lots of time!

Savings and Planning for the Future

So life has changed, and maybe your savings goals have, too. What's important to you now? More travel? School? Starting your own business? What do you want to spend money on? You will be more motivated to save when you have a specific goal in mind than if you are saving simply to have extra money. Plus it's too easy to use an undesignated fund for reasons you hadn't planned on, and then your vacation fund is gone.

Financial advisor Liz Weston has a fresh perspective on budgeting. She advises you make automatic transfers each month to several specific savings accounts named for a particular savings goal. So one account could be labeled "vacation," another "appliances," and a third "car." The specific designation, plus the automatic aspect, makes it easier and more motivating to save. The automatic transfers ensure you are regularly contributing, and it leaves you with your remaining budget for

> You will be more motivated to save when you have a specific goal in mind than if you are saving simply to have extra money. Plus it's too easy to use an undesignated fund for reasons you hadn't planned on, and then your vacation fund is gone.

necessities for that month. It's common to have separate accounts for general saving and investing, but giving specific designations for each account will keep you even more motivated to contribute to the accounts.

As you consider long-term future goals such as college, starting a business, retirement, and wills or bequests, be sure to give yourself enough time to process all of your emotions before you make major decisions. The advice here is to make no changes for six to twelve months. This time gives you a chance to close out your last chapter, fully deal with the emotions of that time, and begin to form goals for the upcoming chapter of your life.

MEAL PLANNING: MAKE MEALS EASY AND FRESH

Meal planning may or may not be new to you. Depending on your situation, you may think you won't need to meal plan in your "new normal" because now you are feeding only yourself. The truth is meal planning is essential for all households, even households of one. It's valuable for three reasons:

1. It ensures you are eating complete, nutritionally balanced meals, which is important to your health.
2. It saves you time by helping you efficiently grocery shop and prepare meals.
3. It saves you money by ensuring you eat all of the food you buy and keeps you from spending money on restaurants and takeout.

If there are other members in your household, meal planning also allows more bonding time by making meals a priority. If you cook a full dinner, everyone is more likely to sit at the table and eat together. And if you include meal planning in your weekly meeting, everyone can help you plan, and the other members of your household will begin to realize the effort and cost of meal preparation.

You don't need to be an outstanding cook (or even a good cook) to meal plan. You can use frozen entrées or cans of soup in your plan. The

Put it Where it Belongs

Eliminate the phrase "I'll put this here for now." Put away items as you use them. You'll turn around one day, and all those "for now" items will have grown into a pile that will take an hour to sort. Smaller is easier to deal with, and you'll barely notice the time spent. Plus clutter attracts other clutter. When you see one out-of-place item on a surface, you instinctively want to put it away. When you see three out-of-place items on a surface, you're more likely to add to the pile instead of putting things away. Don't let clutter get a foothold.

point is simply to create a list of meals you want to eat during the week. Start by listing the meals, then look at your schedule for the week and decide which nights you want to prepare each meal. On busy nights, plan to prepare quick meals. Leave large, time-intensive meals to days when you have more time. Then list all of the ingredients for each meal and make sure you have everything you need. Create a shopping list for the items you don't have.

To remind yourself of what meals are for which days, keep a notepad on your refrigerator. Even if you switch a meal from one day to another, you already have ideas to choose from.

If your household is smaller in size now, you'll need to adjust to cooking for fewer people. Halve recipes, or make the full batch and freeze half to eat on a future evening when you don't have the time (or inclination) to cook. Clearly label your leftovers with the contents and the date prepared, and keep a list on the outside of your freezer and refrigerator so you use up items before they go bad (or clean them out in a timely manner if you can't finish them all).

HOUSEHOLD CHORES AND MAINTENANCE

Some people clear the clutter as they go around the house each day. They pick up things and put them away as soon as they're done with them, or at least at the end of the day. Other people are comfortable leaving things out and perhaps once a week doing a run-through of the house to pick up whatever is out of place. This second approach works okay until a crisis hits or your schedule is suddenly busier than usual. It's easy to skip this weekly decluttering, and then it becomes a monster to deal with.

The best way to ensure your house stays organized and orderly is to do a little maintenance every day. It's easier to tackle a small pile than an overwhelmingly large one. This maintenance could be a five-minute cleanup of your desk space each day or five minutes hanging up clothes or spending five or ten minutes on the mail pile. When you frequently put things away, you spend less cumulative time picking up around the house.

Another option is to select one area of the house each day and spend five to fifteen minutes straightening it. Set a timer if you need to, and when it dings, you're done.

Make it a Routine

For a lasting effect, try to incorporate this "pick-up" time into your morning and evening routines. In the morning, take the time to put away your grooming tools, hang up towels, and put dirty clothes in the laundry. Make your bed and straighten up your nightstand. Unload your dishwasher and put away the clean dishes in the morning so you can put dirty dishes in the dishwasher throughout the day and after your evening meal.

In the afternoon or after work, take a few minutes to sort the mail and throw away junk mail immediately. Place all of your work things in one area so they are ready for the next day. Straighten up the kitchen after dinner. Put all food away. Clear the counters and wipe them down. If you clear the counters every day, it will only take you a minute or two to clean them off, and they will stay clear. People consistently say that clean tabletops and countertops are uplifting. Take five minutes before bed to pick up the living room. Rearrange pillows, fold throw blankets, put the newspaper in the recycling bin, clear off end tables, and put all dishes in the dishwasher or sink.

When you clear surfaces on a daily basis, clutter won't get a foothold. You'll deal with two or three items, which take only a minute to deal with, instead of a huge pile, which will take longer and discourage you from even trying.

Use Containers

Containers will help you keep things organized and help you make the most of shelf space, especially in bathrooms, basements, and garages. Instead of having loose items spread out all along the shelves, put similar items in containers. Under your sinks, divide up items by purpose or whose they are, and use labels.

Keep Less

Keeping less is easier said than done, but it is true that the less we have, the less there is to organize. In her book, *The Other Side of Organized: Finding Balance Between Chaos and Perfection*, Linda Samuels, CPO-CD®, says that we need to acknowledge how much time we spend managing our stuff versus using our stuff. This is so true. Think about coming up with your own set of no-regrets questions (see page 101) so you can let go of more items. With your belongings, find ways to make peace with how much you have and want to have. Everyone's tolerance for stuff and for chaos is a personal choice. Find yours by experimenting.

To keep less, some people set physical boundaries. For example, some might decide to use a dresser drawer as a boundary. They may permit themselves to keep only the number of jeans that will fit into one dresser

Say No

Saying no is an easy way to keep less, but it's often difficult for us to do. You probably have a friend or colleague who has figured out how to say no, with grace. Ask them how they do it. Or try answering the request this way: "What I can do for you is ... but not what you asked." One of my family members used to ask if I wanted this or that item from her home. She was downsizing for an eventual move, but I didn't know that at the time, so I kept saying yes, thinking she had chosen these items just for me. She had, to some extent, but she also was looking for a way to pass on as many items as possible, so I stopped taking every single one she suggested. Instead, I gave her other ideas for where she could give away some of these items I'd refused. And she still loved me even though I said no more often than yes!

drawer. If they buy a new pair, they must donate one of their old pairs to make room. You could limit the number of books you want to read to what will fit on one shelf; more than a shelf full can be overwhelming, and you may appreciate each book less as you speed-read through them, simply because the pile is too large. Other people will use a number, as in, "Each child can have five pairs of pants," or "I need four dresses." A number, to some people, works magically to give them permission to let go.

Make it super-easy to cycle out what you no longer use, want, or love. Except for rotating clothes at the end of seasons, we don't typically have built-in times for cycling out the old and making room for the new. To make it easier, put a box for donations in every closet so you can easily toss in items that don't fit or don't flatter. Set up a box when you bring out holiday décor during the year, and as you buy new, cycle out the old to a person or an organization that will use it and enjoy it.

Observe which toys children and grandchildren play with most frequently. Take out unused toys or books and put them on probation for a while by placing them in a hidden box with an expiration date. If the kids haven't asked for these items by the expiration date (say a month or two), this box can leave your home. The key is to notice what they play with or read most often.

Another way to keep less is to consume less. In the future, when you consider purchasing an item and bringing it into your home, ask yourself some of these questions before you buy it and add it to your household. Bring the list with you!

- How would I use it or where would I wear it?
- Do I already have one?
- Is this how I want to spend my money and/or time?
- Can I borrow this item from someone I know or swap with a friend or family member for this item?
- Does it fit my new life?
- How important is this compared to the space, money, and time it will consume? What's really important to me now?
- Where will I put it? Where will its home be within my house?

Yard Work and Major Upkeep

Use your calendar to record when you need to complete seasonal yard work such as cleaning gutters, changing storm windows, removing holiday decorations, staining a deck, and cleaning or storing patio furniture. In New England, we have to mark our driveways with reflector sticks so snowplow drivers know where the driveway and lawn edges are. We need to get the sticks in the ground before it freezes, which is long before the snow shows up, so I mark this chore on my calendar for late September so I remember to get it done. Write a reminder to yourself regardless of whether you will be performing the work yourself or hiring someone to do it. If you're unsure when the best time is to perform a certain chore, contact a professional in that field and see what he or she recommends.

Mark all routine maintenance calls, such as those for your septic system or heating and air conditioning unit, on your calendar. Most of these service providers have a maintenance plan you can sign up for that will automatically schedule the annual maintenance.

Budget and schedule the larger household improvements. Get estimates for how long your roof will last. Determine when you will need to repaint the exterior of the house. Get all these items down on a list and plot them out over several years to minimize the financial impact and also the interruption to your household.

PAPERWORK: STOP PAPERS FROM TAKING OVER

Paperwork is difficult to stay on top of, mostly because filing seems like such a chore and it's not efficient to file every single day. Still there are ways to easily maintain order with your paperwork. Figure out a time almost every day when you can focus and go through the papers. Do it while you're waiting for dinner to finish cooking, right after breakfast, or during dinner cleanup time. Attach this habit to something you are already in the habit of doing and it will be easier to maintain.

Here are two questions to help you figure out why papers are such an issue for you: What's the root cause? and What creates the paper piles? This is a wonderful use of the Three Ps because there are so many possibilities for what's making papers difficult for you.

> Paperwork is difficult to stay on top of, mostly because filing seems like such a chore and it's not efficient to file every single day.

Weed out the Junk

When you retrieve the mail, immediately flip through it and pull out all of the junk mail.

The Four Ts

I use the Four Ts to process mail and papers.

TIME: Set a regular time for reviewing the papers and making decisions. The papers aren't going away. Address them in a timely manner.

TOOLS: Have the recycle bin, shredder, and calendar nearby as you work on the papers.

TRIAGE: Do it quickly, at least to presort and winnow down to the real decisions that have to be made.

TIE IT UP: Set up files for whatever you're currently working on. Many people carry their current file with them to wherever they work on the mail and paperwork so filing is super-easy. You're eliminating a file pile, or the trip to another room or upstairs. Buy beautiful, inspiring folders for an extra motivational push!

Place the junk mail directly in the recycling before you set the rest of the mail down. If it's information you need to shred, put it in a bag or bin next to your shredder.

Make an Immediate Decision, Even if it's Small

When you first see a piece of paper, maybe you need to slow down to give yourself enough time to make one immediate decision concerning it. Ask yourself: Why can't I move the task on this piece of paper ahead right now? What *else* do I need to know? And then write down that next step directly on the paper or put it on a sticky note attached to the paper. Even if you can't take the next step, you'll know what it needs to be when you review the papers and have the time to do it. You won't waste time figuring out what to do next because you've already done that.

Contain It

Instead of dropping the mail, school-related papers, committee papers, and work papers in a pile on the kitchen table or counter, find a way to contain it such as in a basket or a mail sorter. This container keeps things looking neat, prevents papers from getting lost or shuffled, and makes the papers mobile. You can move the container with you anywhere in the house to address the paperwork and then move it back to its permanent home when you are finished.

Increase Upkeep Efforts

Make it a priority to deal with mail and papers at least one more time weekly than you do now. So if you only tackle things once a week, aim for twice a week. Make progress and downplay the need to be perfect. If you're not used to tackling it every day, but you try to hold yourself to that new schedule, you will burn out and stop all together or become discouraged when you miss a few days in a row.

When you do go through your papers, have your calendar or PDA with you, plus a paper for recording to-do list items and errands. Capture the details on your calendar or lists and toss the paper.

Keep Less to File Less

How can you keep less? Start by knowing how long you should keep important paperwork. You may not need to keep things for as long as you thought. See the chart in the appendix on page 216 for helpful guidelines.

For papers not addressed on this chart, ask yourself: When will I need this again? Why would I need it? Can I get it again somewhere, like online or from another committee member?

Also, set some boundaries on your sentimental paperwork that you keep for scrapbooking, memory albums, and children's artwork/school-work. The limit could be a number or a physical boundary, such as a container. See which one works for you.

Extra Efforts

After you master the basics of maintaining your paperwork, you can take things a step further to become even more organized. Your systems will still function without taking these steps, but they do make things easier for you if you can stick with them.

Presort the piles. Take two minutes a day and presort the paper piles and mail into these basic categories:

- Mine—your own mail
- Yours—belongs to your spouse, partner, or housemate
- Ours—items you want to discuss as a household, such as an invitation or an event

Many companies are eager to go paperless in their billing. Your paper statement will probably have all the information you need to allow you to start receiving the bills electronically.

The benefit of this is that your own pile is smaller and less overwhelming. Put the "ours" pieces on the dinner table, or somewhere nearby, so you can remember to discuss and decide at dinner. One client actually put the items on the empty dinner plate before dinner.

Opt out. This week, when you bring mail into the house, notice the items that you automatically toss out. How can you get off that list or stop that type of mail from coming in? Make one call or send one e-mail to opt out. Next week make another call to opt out of another mailing. Or make one call to receive information electronically instead of on paper. Many companies are eager to go paperless in their billing. Your paper statement will probably have all the information you need to allow you to start receiving the bills electronically. It could be as simple as checking a box on the payment slip.

WHEN LIFE HAPPENS

One of the terms organizers use is backsliding. This is when it's all too much. Something has to give. So much of life is happening that we stop using our systems, maybe for a day or a week or even longer. This is human nature and is probably our own defense mechanism against having too much in our lives. When you stop dealing with your papers for a while or laundry piles up or the counters aren't the way they had been, that's okay. Step back. Figure out what's happening in your life that's taken precedence. Maybe it has to take priority on your energy for a while. And then get back on the wagon, horse, or whatever you call it.

I'd like to give you an example from my life so you'll realize this happens to all of us at some point. Around my fiftieth birthday, I decided to commit to regularly working out at a gym. Before then, I had decided gyms weren't for me because I didn't consider myself athletic or "in shape," and I associated exercise with weight management. Near my birthday, I realized exercise would help me maintain my health and offered far more benefits than weight management. That shift in mindset was key. I valued my health, but wasn't so worried about my weight. When I associated the gym with something I highly valued, I was able to make the gym a higher priority. What can you associate staying organized with in your life so you can give organizing a higher priority?

I was regular with my gym routine for about six months, and then I stopped going. You may find this happens to you with your organizing systems. You may use them faithfully for several months and then one day suddenly want a break. A day off is fine, but when it leads to a week off and then a month off, it can be hard to get back into the habit. That's what happened with me and the gym. I was, however, able to get back to it. You can apply these principles I used to your own struggles, whether it's with paperwork, your craft area, or the kitchen countertops.

1. Set a small goal. I strive for three days a week, not seven or even four. I know myself. Had I said more than three, the first time I fell off the wagon, I'd never get back on. I hope to increase to four, but I'm good with three for now. It's more than zero. Make sure your expectations are realistic.

> The more you are aware of change, the more you can prepare for it and adjust to it.

2. Roll with the unexpected. I cut myself some slack when life crises hit. My housemate went through knee replacement surgery, one and then the other, last summer. A week after the second surgery, my father suffered a heart attack and had quadruple bypass surgery. I *knew* that going to the gym would have burned stress, physically and mentally. But adding one more thing to my to-do list would have caused my head to explode. It's a balance, and I know myself best. If life is throwing you curve balls, live in the moment and cope as best you can, guilt free. Get back to it when life settles back to normal.

3. Remember why you're doing it. Also remember the sense of accomplishment you feel after you complete the task. It's important for me to remember how good I feel after I workout. It makes it easier for me to start. How can you keep this in front of yourself? For me, having a housemate who goes to the gym daily helped because we would talk about her workout, even when I wasn't going. I started missing that feeling, which was a strong motivation. If you don't have someone to discuss your motivation with, try motivating yourself by reflecting on a time when you felt really great about an organizing system. Write that story down and read it frequently.

4. Put it back on your calendar. If I don't plan for it, it doesn't become part of my regular day. It ends up being extra, something that I get to do *if* work is done and *if* the household is all set. I try to make the gym (i.e., me and my health) as important as the household and my business. It's not easy, but as long as the trend heads in the right direction, I'm good with that.

5. Use an accountability partner. It's okay to ask for support. My housemate helps me because I see what going to the gym does for her. A personal trainer, when I first started at the gym, got me motivated and on the right track in just a few sessions. A professional organizer could do the same for you. It doesn't have to be a long relationship. Sometimes it's useful to regularly schedule something. Other times, it's useful just to get a jump start.

As you organized for your fresh start, you likely learned some important new ways to motivate yourself. You understand yourself better now. You found some tips and techniques to stay organized, to whittle down the stuff, and to keep a household organized "enough." It would be useful to write these down or journal about them. This will help instill the ideas and get them into your memory bank for use again.

You've just started a new chapter in life, but eventually this chapter will end and you'll begin yet another chapter. Remember, change is constant, so be flexible. When that next shift happens (and hopefully it won't be for a while), you can reach for this book again and organize another fresh start for those future opportunities. The more you are aware of change, the more you can prepare for it and adjust to it.

Appendix

THE APPENDIX INCLUDES THE QUESTIONNAIRES AND CHARTS I've used throughout the book. These forms also include plenty of blank space so you can record your answers directly in this book. I've included a few key resources; most of yours will be local, coming from trusted family and friends. The "Keep Less" questions are worth bookmarking because you'll come back to them often; you may want to make a photocopy that you can carry with you to help you make a better decision when you are contemplating an impulse buy. You'll also find room to journal about how you would like to spend your time so you can organize your schedule to support your goals, interests, and obligations.

My Goal Definition Worksheet

My goal is:

_____

_____

I'll know I've achieved my goal when:

_____

_____

When I achieve my goal, it will mean … (What will I be able to do?)

_____

_____

This goal reflects the following important value(s) for me:

_____

_____

What metaphor resonates with me? As I begin my fresh start with this goal, I expect things to look and feel like this:

_____

_____

And when I achieve this goal, the metaphor I identify with will be:

_____

_____

Not achieving this goal will have these negative consequences:

_____

_____

The attitudes and internal clutter holding me back that I need to shift or let go of are:

_____

_____

Which external clutter challenges will be difficult? Which will be easy?

_____

_____

I have the following external support systems available to help me now:

_____

_____

I will support myself while reaching this goal by ... (self-care: sleep, exercise, rewards, etc.)

_____

_____

Developed by Susan Fay West and Kathryn May, Life by Intention

Clearing the Clouds of Confusion Exercise

Transitions can leave your thoughts in a fog of confusion. Things have changed, and you may feel like aspects of your life are out of control. This exercise will help you identify the aspects of your life that you are satisfied with and the aspects of your life that you want to improve. You will need a pen and a stack of index cards or sticky notes.

Consider the components of your life. Examples could be:

Family/Children	Self-Care/Exercise	Social/Friends
Family/Partner	Self-Care/Medical	Social/Romantic
Family/Parents	Job/Career	Social/Clubs
Living Situation	Finances/Short-Term	Hobbies/Creativity
Self-Care/Rest	Finances/Long-Term	Spirituality
Self-Care/Diet	Finances/Retirement Plan	

1. Write one component per index card. Make as many as you need and add components specific to your life.

2. Arrange the index cards so the components are placed in order from what you are most satisfied to least satisfied with. You could rank them A, B, C, etc., or give each a ranking between one and ten. Even if you are dissatisfied with everything, some things will be better than others. Rank them honestly. You may find you are more satisfied than you thought.

3. Focus on the bottom three components. Decide why you are dissatisfied. Then decide whether you'd like to identify steps you can take to change this or if you'd like to make some of the strong areas even stronger. Then work your way around the list until you are satisfied with every aspect of your life.

Suggested Reading List

The E-Myth Revisited: Why Most Small Businesses Don't Work and What to Do About It by Michael E. Gerber. Published by HarperCollins.

I Could Do Anything If I Only Knew What it Was: How to Discover What You Really Want and How to Get It by Barbara Sher and Barbara Smith. Published by Dell.

Organizing for the Creative Person: Right-Brain Styles for Conquering Clutter, Mastering Time, and Reaching Your Goals by Dorothy Lehmkuhl and Dolores Cotter Lamping. Published by Three Rivers Press.

Simple Abundance by Sarah Ban Breathnach. Published by Warner Books.

What's Next: Women Redefining Their Dreams in the Prime of Life by Rena Pederson. Published by Cahners Business Information, Inc.

Room Tour Questions

What do you see? _____

What do people comment on when they arrive? _____

What kind of energy do you feel in this spot? _____

What's in place? Out of place? _____

How would you like this space to be? _____

What activities go on here? _____

What activities used to occur here but don't anymore (but the stuff is still located here)? And what activities would you like to have happen here but don't today because of clutter or space or other considerations?

_____

_____

What frustrates you about this area? _____

Do you enjoy the color scheme? _____

What systems are important to have here and are they working for you today? (Sometimes it is helpful to answer this with a 1–10 scale, 10 being perfect. Usually, some parts of the system are working; it's not the whole system that's failed you.)

_____

_____

Keep Less Questions

Put a copy of this list in your purse or wallet and consult it when you consider purchasing an item and bringing it into your home.

How would I use it or where would I wear it?

_____

Do I already have one?

_____

Is this how I want to spend my money and/or time?

_____

Can I borrow this item from someone I know or swap with a friend or family member for this item?

_____

Does it fit my new life?

_____

How important is this compared to the space, money, and time it will consume? What's really important to me now?

_____

Where will I put it? Where will its home be within my house?

_____

Home is Not Home Without Chart

ROOM	HOME IS NOT HOME WITHOUT...
Hallway or Entryway	
Bedroom 2	
Bedroom 3	
Bedroom 4 or Office	
Master Bedroom	
Kitchen	
Laundry Area	
Dining Room	

ROOM	HOME IS NOT HOME WITHOUT...
Home Office	
Bathroom	
Living Room	
Den	
Attic	
Basement	
Garage/Shed	

Decluttering Your Calendar

What would you rather be doing with your time? This question identifies your values, which will help you make clearer choices when you have scheduling conflicts.

Paint the full picture. Identify all of the things you must do and all of the things you want to do. How much time will it all take? What will you need to give up?

Identify what and who saps your energy. Decline or delegate tasks you dread.

Wear your hats well. Draw an organizational chart of your work life and then of your home life. Which roles are you best at? Keep these. Consider removing or mitigating the others, things you don't do well or put off, from your schedule.

Chunk it down. What's the smallest step you can take so you can get started on the task right away? It's easier to fit in small steps, and you can make steady progress.

Anchor yourself. David Allen pioneered the idea of a weekly review for the workplace in his book *Getting Things Done*. The weekly review idea is also useful with your personal life. Toward the end of the week, set aside thirty minutes to review your life for the upcoming week.

Keep track of time. Use a clock or timer to track how long it takes you to accomplish your everyday tasks. Record these times electronically or on paper. Then use this information to accurately understand how time passes as well as to budget your time. Always give yourself a fifteen-minute cushion to account for interruptions or delays.

Instead of one more thing, do one less thing. I used to be the one running into meetings right on time (sometimes late) or getting to a friend's house late for dinner. Why? Because I was doing "just one more thing" before I'd leave the house or office. Now I do one less thing, and guess what, the task I left undone is still waiting for me when I return.

Identify How You Would Like to Spend Your Time

These are the key questions to ask yourself as you decide what to do and how to spend your time in your next chapter. Take time to journal about each of these questions.

What do you value? What is important now?

_____

_____

_____

_____

_____

Where are you doing the best in your life or living the best version of you? What's working well?

_____

_____

_____

_____

_____

Which facet of your life would you like to improve?

_____

_____

_____

_____

What do you currently know about what you want next, no matter how small you may think it sounds?

_____

_____

_____

_____

_____

What do you know about your vision or about your ideas for your next chapter? Write it, paint it, say it aloud—whatever works to keep it alive.

_____

_____

_____

_____

What is holding you back internally?

_____

_____

_____

_____

_____

What do you need to let go of? What makes it difficult to let go? What do you need or what questions can you ask yourself to make a no-regrets decision and move on?

What is important to keep with you going forward? What is now permanently part of your being, your core, your essence?

What has this life event taught you about yourself?

How can that new information help you create your next chapter?

_____

_____

_____

_____

_____

_____

How have you created something from nothing (or very little) in the past? What principles, ideas, or actions from that experience can you apply to this new experience?

_____

_____

_____

_____

_____

What are the major accomplishments in your life? How did you approach and achieve them?

_____

_____

_____

_____

_____

_____

What is one goal you can limit yourself to for now? It's important to start and finish one goal and then move on to another. If you start several at once, it's difficult to sustain momentum because your first success takes longer. A success, no matter how small, feeds you.

_____

_____

_____

_____

_____

How will you know when you have achieved that one goal? How will you realize it, feel it, or see it? What does it look like or feel like when you've achieved the goal?

_____

_____

_____

_____

What are the smallest steps you can take to begin chipping away at your goal?

_____

_____

_____

_____

_____

How Long to Keep Records

RECORD	KEEP FOR	REASON
Taxes	seven years	The IRS has three years from your filing date to audit your return if it suspects good-faith errors. It has six years to challenge your return if it thinks you under-reported your gross income by 25 percent or more. There is no time limit if you failed to file your return or filed a fraudulent return. You also have three years to file an amended return to claim a refund if you discover a mistake in your return.
Bank Statements	one month to permanently	Balance your ledger each month. Go through your checks each month and keep those related to your taxes, business expenses, home improvements, and mortgage payments. Shred those that have no long-term importance.
Bills	one month	Keep the most current statement. Shred the previous month's when the new arrives unless you are tracking your expenses for budgeting reasons.
Credit Card Receipts & Statements	45 days to seven years	Keep your original receipts until you get your monthly statement; shred the receipts if the two match up. Keep the statements for seven years if tax-related expenses are documented; otherwise keep only the most current statement.
Paycheck Stubs	one year	When you receive your annual W-2 form from your employer, make sure the information on your stubs matches. If it does, shred the stubs. If it doesn't, demand a corrected form, known as a W-2c.
Receipts for Major Expenses	length of ownership	Keep these receipts in an insurance file for proof of their value in the event of loss or damage. Major expenses include jewelry, rugs, appliances, antiques, cars, collectibles, furniture, computers, and electronics.